Barrier Breaker
Be Yourself Bril.

Penelope Tobin

DODGEM

London

Published by Dodgem
74a Woodland Gardens,
London N10 3UB
United Kingdom
P: 020 8292 0991
E: byb@dodgem.org.uk

Produced for Dodgem by Lightning Source
Copy-edited by Sylvia Worth

British Library Cataloguing in Publication Data
A catalogue record for this book is available from the British Library

ISBN 978-0-9565701-0-9

Grateful acknowledgment is made to the following for their permission to reproduce copyright
material:
Coleman Barks for "The Guest House", from *The Essential Rumi*.
Beyond Words Publishing, Hillsboro, Oregon for "Autobiography in Five Short Chapters", from
There's a Hole in my Sidewalk, Portia Nelson.
The Anais Nin Trust for "Trust" by Anais Nin.
Peter Firebrace for "Cool Rule".
Richard Hill for "Shadow Man".
The publishers and the Trustees of Amherst College for "Each Life Converges", from *The Poems of
Emily Dickinson*, Thomas H. Johnson, ed., Cambridge, Mass.: The Belknap Press of Harvard Univer-
sity Press, Copyright © 1951, 1955, 1979, 1983 by the President and Fellows of Harvard College
Faber and Faber for "Little Gidding", from *Collected Poems 1909-1962*, T.S.Eliot. [pending]

To the trustees, volunteers, funders and friends
who have supported Barrier Breakers.
Thank you for making it possible.

Contents

brilliantly!

Be yourself, because everyone else is already taken

OSCAR WILDE

How To Use This Book

Barrier Breakers: Be Yourself Brilliantly! is based on Barrier Breakers Methodology (BBM), a unique approach to personal and professional development. Since 2002 BBM has helped many hundreds of individuals and organisations; it's used in numerous programmes, from confidence building for students through to communication training for company directors; it's applied to executive coaching and it enables ex-offenders to develop life skills; it won a national award for its contribution to the performance of voluntary sector organisations; it helps graduates make career choices, the recently redundant find a new path, entrepreneurs build their businesses, and employers make the most of their people.

If you'd like to get an overall sense of what the BBM process entails, then leap in and read the book straight through. Then immerse yourself in each chapter, take plenty of time to consider the content, don't rush, allow your thoughts to percolate, and complete the exercises.

Do this, and you will achieve whatever changes you wish to make. You'll break through the barriers that hold you back from making the most of yourself and from enjoying life to the full.

> *Even if you're on the right track*
> *you'll get run over if you just sit there*
>
> **WILL ROGERS**

Before setting off, there are a few suggestions for how to get the most out of the book. But first, an apology to the grammar pedants among you. Instead of using 'his' and/or 'her' I've chosen to use 'their'—bad English some say, but good sense, succinct and gender neutral I say!

Using a journal to track your experience is highly recommended—suggestions for how to use one are detailed in the first exercise. There's *The Journal* that accompanies this book, or you can create your own.

Some barriers may seem less relevant to you, but these could be the very ones that hold the biggest clues. If you find yourself rapidly dismissing something, give it a second look.

> *You must do the thing*
> *you think you cannot do*
>
> **ELEANOR ROOSEVELT**

During many years of researching, developing, and applying BBM, everyone I've worked with has found its approach easy to project onto their life, using it as a lens through which to look at their unique circumstances. Introducing case studies and anecdotes can be a handy short cut to understanding, but in the long run these seem to place limits on how BBM is interpreted. I hope the lack of other people's stories, including my own, helps you to focus BBM more directly onto your life, so you can see your unique story with greater clarity.

We are all special cases

ALBERT CAMUS

BBM is simple…it's been called 'codified common sense'…but still, please be patient with yourself. Take your time to get familiar with BBM, absorb it, play with the ideas, make mistakes, experiment with the exercises, forget things, repeat things, and mull over the poems and quotes. Let BBM work for you, and let your progress take its own time and course.

You'll find information about BBM training programmes as well as additional resources at www.barrierbreakers.co.uk.

BBM gives you all the tools you need to break through the barriers in your life—but you've still got to take the action yourself. That's the work no one else can do! However, this book has been written to make your adventure easier and more enjoyable. And I'm honoured that you've chosen to make *Barrier Breakers: Be Yourself Brilliantly!* a companion on your journey.

You will do foolish things,
but do them with enthusiasm

COLETTE

Introduction

Imagine you're driving…

You're at the wheel, in control of your journey, looking ahead with your destination in mind, yet also enjoying the scenery along the way. You're looking forward, while keeping an eye on what's going on around you.

You glance in the rear view mirror: **backward focus** lets you know what's behind you, and how that could affect what's happening now and up ahead.

How you're feeling in yourself is important: **inward focus** makes sure you're alert and in the best frame of mind for travelling.

You notice what the road conditions are like: **downward focus** tells you what's underlying your journey, what you can sense but can't see.

And then your peripheral vision lets you know what's going on around you: **left focus** and **right focus** give you a full, rich perspective of the scenery you're travelling through.

When you're looking ahead, while being 'in the moment' and informed by everything around you, you have what's called **forward focus**. This focus is the one that makes your journey as relaxed, successful and enjoyable as possible.

And life's a journey.

> A good traveller has no fixed plans
> And is not intent upon arriving
>
> LAO-TZU

However…

What happens if your attention is drawn away from forward focus?

How will your journey be affected if another focus distracts you for too long?

When a focus that's meant to inform your journey becomes the one directing your journey it will distract you rather than support you; it will block your progress rather than allow you to move forward with ease; it will dominate you rather allowing you to be in balance. In short, it will become a barrier.

Barrier Breakers: Be Yourself Brilliantly! shows you how to break through the barriers, to achieve forward focus and make the journey of your life a joyful, rewarding adventure.

You will:

- **Explore** the five focuses that can become barriers to your progress—backward focus, inward focus, downward focus, left focus, and right focus—and find out how each barrier blocks your potential.
- **Assess** whether these barriers are showing up in your life, so you can identify them in yourself and in others, and see where they're holding you back from being your best and enjoying your journey to the maximum.
- **Shift** the barriers. You'll get specific techniques to achieve this, and learn how to design and apply them directly to your unique circumstances.
- **Transform** each barrier, so every focus is in balance and you can move ahead with a forward focus.

When you've completed *Barrier Breakers: Be Yourself Brilliantly!* you'll be able to travel with purpose and energy, guided by your intuition and creativity; to recognise barriers when they arise and be ready to break through them; to move towards your goals, but not be bound by them; to look forward while living fully in the moment.

1 Preparing For The Journey, Priming For Change

This book aims to support you make whatever changes you want to make in your life, by identifying and overcoming the barriers that stand in your way. It gives you a simple, powerful strategy that you can use to:

- Make more of yourself—if you feel you're not making the most of yourself, and would like to identify and overcome what's holding you back.
- Make changes—if you want to make a particular change in your life, and would like to prepare for it by removing anything that could get in the way of your success.

Perhaps you know you're not using all of your talents and capabilities, but can't put your finger on what's stopping you. You want to grow personally and professionally but feel stuck. You've achieved some goals, but they haven't brought you the joy you expected. Or you've self-sabotaged your goals and don't know why you're wasting time. You want to turn things around.

If you feel you're not living up to your potential, it's because you know instinctively that you've a wealth of ability you're not tapping into; you've got it, but you can't get to it.

> We are all functioning
> at a small fraction of our capacity
>
> **WINSTON CHURCHILL**

BBM defines the five barriers that block all potential and gives you the means to break through them. It shows you how to access your own wisdom and capabilities, by identifying and removing internal and external barriers.

You already have all you need to succeed. You don't need more input from an expert—you just need to be able to get hold of what you already have and make the most of it. And that's what BBM helps you to do.

> *The mind is not an empty vessel to be filled*
> *but a fire to be ignited*
>
> **PLUTARCH**

Perhaps there's a specific change you want to make, but despite your best intentions it's just not happening. Many of us want to make changes. We might be determined, even desperate. Need for change could be urgent. Perhaps the techniques we've found to help us make the change seem extremely promising. And yet all too often the change, if it happens at all, is temporary. We find ourselves back on a familiar path, even more frustrated and disillusioned than before. We tried our best, and yet we failed.

> Much of what firms do
> in the name of strategic planning
> is no more effective
> than individuals making New Year's resolutions
>
> DAVID MAISTER

Although many personal and professional change plans are promising, they often fail because one vital step is omitted.

This book provides that step. It shows you how to 'prime' for change before you attempt to make a change. Think of it like this…if you want to redecorate your home, you know that first you need to do the 'prep', to make ready, to get the necessary tools together, to fill, sand, wash…to prime the surfaces. If you don't prepare in this way, neither the effort you put into it, nor the quality of materials you use, will make the end result as good or long-lasting as it could be. It may look lovely for a while…but soon the paint peels away, it looks terrible, and you're in a bigger mess than when you started.

Similarly, before we make changes to any part of our lives, we need to 'prime' ourselves and the situation. *Barrier Breakers: Be Yourself Brilliantly!* is the primer you need to prepare for any change. It helps you to identify and remove problem areas, the potential pitfalls, the barriers. Yes, these can be lumpy and stubborn and unattractive, and most of us prefer to get on with the painting! But priming is crucial to success. Like the foundation of a building, you may not win prizes for it, but you certainly won't win prizes without it; everything else depends on it, and if you don't take care of it everything else will collapse.

BBM makes 'priming' enjoyable, and the outcome deeply rewarding. It gives you a secure foundation from which to launch any change, and whatever 'redecorating materials' you then use, the end result is the long-term success you seek.

Before setting off into this book, consider a change you'd like to make. You don't need to have a clear idea at present. There may be something specific you want to do, or you may have a more general desire to find out whether barriers are holding you back. You may know exactly what you want to achieve, or only have the vaguest feeling that things aren't right. Whatever it is, for now just keep it in mind, and allow it to evolve as it wishes.

> *Trust that still, small voice that says,*
> *this might work and I'll try it*
>
> **DIANE MARIECHILD**

By the time you reach Chapter 4 you'll have a clearer idea of the change you'd like this book to help you make. So from thereon, let this idea be the springboard for your thoughts and actions. Use it as the basis for the exercises. Put it through the BBM process. However, be flexible, keep an open mind, and take risks—it's very possible that your change plan will change as barriers get broken!

Your adventure begins here…

Risk

by Anais Nin

And then the day came,
when the risk
to remain tight
in a bud
was more painful
than the risk
it took
to Blossom

2 The Five Barriers

Introduction

We are born full of curiosity, noticing everything around us, soaking up information, learning at an incredible pace, reaching out to explore anything that comes our way, highly creative and playful, unconditionally loving, and fully involved in the moment.

Is that what you're like today?

What happens to our enquiring spirit, our lust for learning, our natural individuality, our ability to play spontaneously and express our emotions easily, our sense of connection to others, our pleasure in being alive and being ourselves?

In the western world we have countless blessings, yet we are epidemically unhappy. Our material abundance seems to bring remarkably little joy, especially considering the time and energy we expend on it, the sacrifices we make for it, and the importance we attach to it. We strive constantly for more and all that is bigger, better and faster, incapable of arriving at a point of satiation. And amid the frenzy we lose sight of the very attributes that actually make us happy.

*Happiness is not a matter of intensity
but of balance and order
and rhythm and harmony*

THOMAS MERTON

The attributes upon which our happiness depends are inherent human capabilities. They exist within us all. They don't require special knowledge, aptitude, talent or intelligence. They can never vanish completely. But they can fade, underrated and almost forgotten, buried beneath what are seen to be weightier, more important matters.

These attributes are known as **soft skills**—defined in BBM as the "traits and abilities of attitude and behaviour rather than knowledge or technical aptitude". Soft skills, such as communication, creativity, empathy and leadership, determine how we experience life; they are our essence, the root of our potential, the spring of our happiness, our humanity.

*The soft stuff is always harder
than the hard stuff*

ROGER ENRICO

It's not only as individuals that we suffer when our soft skills aren't valued or developed, but also as a society.

*The great paradox is that,
in this age of powerful technology,
the biggest problems we face internationally
are problems of the human soul*

RALPH PETERS

Even though they're now widely recognised as crucial determinants of social and economic development, soft skills are still sidelined in our education system and, despite the lip service, are generally treated as add-ons in the business world.

When you rediscover and develop these skills in yourself, you'll find a treasure trove of tools with which to navigate the life you choose, to meet its inevitable challenges head on, to connect with others, to follow your dreams, and to love the adventure.

*The future belongs to those who believe
in the beauty of their dreams*

ELEANOR ROOSEVELT

To reach this wealth of potential there are just five barriers to overcome; subsequent chapters go into each barrier in detail. The following brief descriptions introduce you to the barriers, tell you something of their characteristics, and outline the benefits you'll gain by breaking through each of them.

Backward Focus

Breaking through the barrier of backward focus shifts your attention away from past influences. This includes your own experience, which can make you relive your past and turn it into your future, as well as the influence of your family and culture—in other words, the indoctrination you receive from forces outside yourself. Living to satisfy others' expectations distances you from your true self.

> **Don't waste your time**
> **Living someone else's life**
> **Don't be trapped by dogma**
> **Living with the results**
> **Of other people's thinking**
> **STEVE JOBS**

Breaking through backward focus allows the past to inform you without dominating you, helping you realign yourself to who you really are, what you believe, what your purpose is, and what you want from life.

BBM has a 'non-deficit' approach—rather than suggesting we lack anything, it proposes that we have immeasurable, unknown and untapped capabilities, limited only by the barriers that we and others construct.

From an early age we're used to being labelled; it feels normal, real even. And there are many experts who add weight to this illusion. They can tell you everything about yourself, and then use their definition of you to specify how you can be improved. For example, there's now a multitude of tests that pick apart every facet of your personality. These are widely used; they're accepted practice in numerous organisations. But if you define your personality by the results of a test, you're putting false limitations on yourself, based entirely on another's criteria. If you wish to live within such limitations it's a matter of choice, but it's not a matter of fact. How could it be, when there's so much we don't understand about ourselves, our minds, our world, our universe?

Breaking through backward focus is about making the choice not to be limited by 'boxes', and instead to find opportunities to develop your own thinking through **self-referring approaches**. This means:

- reflecting on and questioning accepted thinking in yourself and others
- being adaptable rather than automatically sticking to a well-trodden path
- being self-reliant and using your initiative rather than leaning on others by default
- developing your leadership qualities in whatever capacity is needed, not least the ability to lead your own life.

*Do not rely completely
on any other human being, however dear.
We meet all life's greatest tests alone*

AGNES MACPHAIL

Even as we're travelling with many others, life is essentially a solitary journey. From Confucius to Buckaroo Banzai, sages through the ages have noted, "wherever you go, there you are". Breaking through backward focus allows you access to your own inner strength whenever you need it. This gives you genuine security.

Inward Focus

Breaking through the barrier of inward focus shifts your attention away from yourself, and out onto the part you play in the bigger picture—the impact you have on others, the world around you, and your life in the longer term.

Breaking through inward focus removes you from the trap of a narcissistic, short-term world view—yours or others'—and helps you to establish supportive relationships, healthy communication channels, and a stronger sense of connection.

> *As individuals and as a nation,*
> *we now suffer from social narcissism*
>
> **DANIEL J. BOORSTI**

The barrier of inward focus doesn't only afflict individuals, but also families, communities, organisations, religions, governments, and countries.

Some consider this is one of the biggest, most devastating issues of the day, with the self-centredness and entitlement that it breeds producing problems through-out society: from a general lack of care for others, to all abusive relationships; from self-serving corporate cultures, such as the financial institutions and global corporations that cause widespread damage without a blink of remorse, to the political and religious ideologues who never doubt their entitlement to inflict their world view on everyone else.

You may identify that inward focus is driving your own behaviour, and this you can address; you may also realise that you're dealing with it elsewhere in your life and, while you can't change others' behaviour, seeing it clearly for what it is means you're able to change your response to it.

Breaking through inward focus is about developing **empathic approaches**. This means you increase your awareness of others' circumstances, and are able to reflect on situations from their perspective.

> *The great gift of human beings*
> *is that we have the power of empathy*
> MERYL STREEP

Being more interested in and aware of another's position makes you better at social interaction, improving general communication as well as specific skills, such as negotiating and networking. It also means you're tuned in to any manipulative or controlling behaviour in your environment, and positioned to deal with it. You become a better listener and use words more wisely; you hear others' true meaning without clouding it with your own thoughts, and you communicate your true meaning more coherently to others. It's about being connected—sharing yourself, collaborating, presenting your ideas, working as part of a team.

Shifting your attention away from yourself gives you a fuller perspective, making it easier to take the long view and see the full impact of your actions. This allows you to develop a natural patience, rather than being limited to a need for immediate gratification.

*We live in a culture
that discourages empathy.
A culture that too often tells us
our principle goal in life
is to be rich, thin, young,
famous, safe, and entertained*

BARACK OBAMA

Breaking through inward focus improves all your relationships, increasing your ability to communicate effectively. It also allows you to recognise when this destructive barrier is emanating from others, and to take the necessary action to avoid its impact.

Downward Focus

Breaking through the barrier of downward focus shifts your attention away from the shadow side of life, so you'll no longer be dominated by underlying fears or anxieties. Shining a light onto this more mysterious, elusive side allows you to put it to positive use in your life. Breaking through downward focus gives you access to your inner wisdom through your intuition, gut reactions, and dreams.

In a dark time, the eye begins to see;
I meet my shadow in the deepening shade

ROETHKE

In BBM, the term **shadow** is used to describe the hidden part of any person or situation, which is either denied or not recognised. Although it has a far broader interpretation in BBM, shadow is not dissimilar in meaning to the archetype in Jungian psychology that describes the unconscious part of our psyche.

The shadow isn't necessarily dark in character, but it may have become associated with something shameful. Perhaps a learnt belief that anger is bad disallows you from using anger appropriately; or maybe your parent was a strict perfectionist and you now fear making any mistakes.

The shadow can control us, and we can become unwittingly habituated to emotions that dominate our lives. The shadow can also submerge our most positive qualities, the psyche guarding them for its own convoluted reason. This is the covert and complicated nature of Downward Focus, the hardest of the five barriers to identify. It's not only difficult to recognise in ourselves, but also in others; those with the most aggressive shadow side may wear the gentlest mask. However, it's crucial to recognise the shadow in others as well as in ourselves, and BBM offers ways to shine a light onto it.

To overcome downward focus use **trust approaches**; these are concerned primarily with trusting yourself and your inner wisdom, by paying attention to and respecting your intuitive responses.

I shut my eyes in order to see
PAUL GAUGIN

Too often we dismiss our instincts: we 'should' like that seemingly charming person; we 'ought to' be grateful for the job everyone tells us is amazing; we're 'wrong' to be miserable in our relationship. However, when you listen to your inner voice you are given a very accurate account of a situation; it works in tandem with your gut reaction to tell you exactly what's right for you. The barrier of downward focus can only exist when the shadow is denied. By trusting your responses, and paying attention to the shadow side, you remove the barrier, and can then access the shadow's beneficial power.

Intensity is silent,
its image is not.
I love everything that dazzles me
and then accentuates the darkness within me

RENE CHAR

Being aware of downward focus allows you to recognise when its attempts to control you are coming from external sources—such as from manipulators or 'emotional vampires'—as well as from your own inner machinations. Hiding things from yourself is debilitating, and making sure your mask is in place demands a lot of attention; when this is no longer necessary, defensiveness drops away and concentration comes more easily. Accepting yourself in all your complexity means you're more comfortable in your own skin. This increases genuine self-confidence and your ability to be assertive. Motivation springs from this positive attitude; so begins a virtuous circle. Downward focus is the most challenging barrier to overcome, but it's also the most worthwhile—our darkest shadow contains our most brilliant possibility.

Left Focus

Breaking through the barrier of left focus shifts your attention away from the overuse of logic, so you won't let reason judge your ideas too soon, or stop you attempting to achieve your dreams. Breaking through left focus means you have a better balance between your ability to analyse and rationalise, and your ability to imagine and create.

Starting with our education, and stretching throughout our working lives, we are taught that the only really credible way of determining worth is by measuring it numerically. We assess our early progress through marks in exams; we work to achieve specific targets and measurable outcomes; we value people according to their income. Left focus applauds this attitude; it understands this idea of logic.

And because it's so widespread we all become adapted to this way of being; anything less tangible seems airy-fairy, wishy-washy, even downright weird.

However, there's an increasingly common strand of thought that questions this accepted paradigm, proposing that for individual and collective well-being the quantitative must be balanced by the qualitative, the tangible by the intangible; and ever more so in a world where the only certainty is change.

All of those numbers
are making us misunderstand things
DAVID BOYLE

BBM has been created from a passionate conviction that soft skills are an immensely valuable yet sorely underused resource. They're paid scant attention, not because their value isn't known, but because they don't suit left focus, particularly with regard to measurement. The BBM assessment process, which is used in education and training contexts, has been designed to address this problem—producing data that satisfies left focus, while still respecting and retaining the true characteristics of these essential yet elusive skills.

Breaking through left focus is about developing **intuitive approaches**, to give the 'other' side of your brain a workout, by flexing your muscles of play, adventure, and creativity. So you explore creative techniques to tease your mind out of its ruts, and you set up the best environments to generate numerous ideas, allowing your intuition and imagination to come up with solutions, without left focus imme-diately critiquing them or setting expectations. Your individuality thrives under these conditions, increasing the likelihood of original thought—the best mode of thinking when dealing with rapid change.

36

> *Imagination, not invention,*
> *is the supreme master of art, as of life*
>
> JOSEPH CONRAD

This is also the key to effective problem solving, for while left focus has a role to play here, it won't get off the starting block without creativity. Similarly with innovation; when creativity moves towards function then left focus makes a good partner, but only once the ideas have been allowed to flow, unrestricted. Breaking through left focus allows you to escape the one-dimentional rule of numbers, to develop a richer concept of value and worth, to explore your creativity and individuality, and to be better prepared for making and taking on change.

Right Focus

Breaking though the barrier of right focus shifts your attention away from your imagination, so you can frame your ideas in the best way to bring them to life, and structure your activities to make the most of your time and energy. Breaking through right focus means you move thoughts into action, theory into practice, ideas into substance.

Most of us haven't been encouraged to overuse our imagination, as beyond early childhood it's not something that features strongly in our education, nor is it considered to be a substantial element of good parenting. However, ironically, while imagination doesn't feature strongly in our upbringing, neither do the skills that we need to structure our lives effectively. Perhaps this is due to the outmoded expectation that all but a select few of us will be working for someone else, within someone else's structure. However, workers have moved out of the predictable routine, common in the twentieth century, into a far more unstable environment. Now we all need to be able to sculpt our own lives.

Think not of yourself
as the architect of your career
but as the sculptor.
Expect to have to do
a lot of hard hammering
and chiselling and scraping and polishing

B C FORBES

Many people berate themselves for being disorganised, lazy, forgetful, or bad at managing their time, when in reality these are not the problem, merely the symptoms. It's not some inherent personality defect that's causing them to live chaotically; they've simply not acquired the necessary skills, nor found the systems that work for them.

I must create a system
or be enslaved by another man's

WILLIAM BLAKE

Right focus will try to persuade you that setting up systems is dull, uncreative, no fun, only for really boring people. But hunting for stuff is dull; always running late isn't creative; having your finances in a mess is not fun; and lacking direction in life is boring.

Breaking through right focus is about integrating **structured approaches** into your life. The secret to success in this is quite straightforward—find the systems and structures that you get pleasure from doing, that suit your circumstances and personal style, and that lead you towards the things that really excite you. Once you've designed structures you enjoy, it's no longer about self discipline—it's about setting yourself up to get as much out of the process as the outcome.

The more I want to get something done, the less I call it work

RICHARD BACK

When you're in control of your systems you organise your activities easily, manage your time efficiently, and put your ideas into action. You remember things, make decisions, and plan; you have clarity about the direction you're going in, rather than being blown about randomly like a feather in the breeze.

Breaking through right focus clears clutter from your life and creates space in your mind, allowing you to design the best route to get you where you want to go.

Summary

These five barriers block all human potential. Break through the barriers, and you access your innate abilities, your soft skills, your inherent competencies. These are the supplies you need for a joyful, purposeful journey.

Breaking through these barriers gives you the balance of forward focus, where you're informed by all five focuses and dominated by none; where you look ahead while living fully in the moment.

Each of the following chapters is dedicated to one of the barriers, and leads you through the BBM process of Explore, Assess, Shift, Transform—EAST. This process, which is discussed in the next chapter, is deceptively powerful. Don't be perturbed if you unearth some challenging issues as you dig for your treasure; breaking barriers can involve some shovelling! But the rewards are so valuable that you'll want to do it.

Take it at your own pace, have time-out if you'd like to absorb the changes you're making, and get further support if you need to. But, above all else...

...have fun!

Laughter is the tonic,
the relief,
the surcease for pain

CHARLIE CHAPLIN

The Guest House

by Rumi

This being human is a guest house.

Every morning a new arrival.

A joy, a depression, a meanness,

some momentary awareness comes

as an unexpected visitor.

Welcome and entertain them all!

Even if they're a crowd of sorrows,

who violently sweep your house

empty of its furniture,

still, treat each guest honourably.

He may be clearing you out

for some new delight.

The dark thought, the shame, the malice,

meet them at the door laughing,

and invite them in.

Be grateful for whoever comes,

because each has been sent

as a guide from beyond.

translation by Coleman Barks

3 The BBM Process

Explore, Assess, Shift, Transfo.

Introduction

In the upcoming chapters you'll be looking at the five focuses in turn, to understand how each focus becomes a barrier, identify whether this barrier is present in your life, and learn how to break through the barrier. To do this you'll be using the BBM process **EAST** which comprises four stages—Explore, Asses, Shift, Transform. Here is an explanation of how EAST works, and what you can expect from each stage.

Explore

This stage introduces the **dominant influence** of each focus—what it is about that particular focus that draws your attention; for example, backward focus has the dominant influence of past, and you'll explore what that means, and how it affects you.

A dominant influence is not inherently negative; in fact it's essential to your well-being and can be developed in its own right. But if a dominant influence draws too much of your attention, it will throw you out of balance with forward focus, producing a barrier with distinctive characteristics and effects.

.his book is concerned with how barriers affect you as an individual, but

 arriers also influence groups, organisations and society more broadly, and that's

touched upon at this stage, to give you a flavour of the bigger picture.

Assess

The second stage gives you an opportunity to consider where each barrier could be

showing up in your life, and outlines various indicators, or **inhibitors**, that point to

it. These inhibitors are so called because they inhibit, or block, the skills you already

possess, which limits your ability and reduces your potential.

There are a lot of questions at this stage, designed to prod your thinking.

Initially, answer the questions spontaneously, almost as if the answers were already

there as part of the text. This way you'll build an instinctive sketch of the focus as

it appears in your life, which will reveal whether it's become a barrier.

> *I think self-awareness is probably the most important thing towards being a champion*
>
> **BILLIE JEAN KING**

Once you've completed the chapter, come back to the questions and give

more thought to your responses. Not only will your revised answers be of interest

in themselves, but they'll also uncover any habitual thinking patterns you have—

automatic responses, prejudices, assumptions, things you're defensive about, or

things you don't give yourself enough credit for.

44

Shift

The third stage introduces the **counteracting approach** that you'll use if any focus has become a barrier, to shift your attention away from the dominiating influence and back into balance with forward focus. Each focus is associated to a particular type of counteracting approach, but within this there are infinite variations. Those offered here are general ones to use while reading the book; once you've grasped the simple principles behind them you'll be able to create your own counteracting approaches, to suit your particular circumstances.

Try to complete all the counteracting approaches in a chapter before moving on to consider a new focus. This will give you enough time to get to know each focus and its counteracting approach, to absorb the concepts, play with the ideas, assess whether the focus has become a barrier, shift your thinking, and make changes.

Transform

The fourth and final stage details the positive effect that shifting the barrier has, specifically the soft skills you'll access and be able to develop.

In BBM, soft skills are defined as "skills of attitude and behaviour rather than knowledge or technical aptitude"—the skills that determine how you do whatever you do. You don't need any expert to teach these skills to you—you have them already. They're innate human competencies. If you're not using them, it's not because you don't have them, it's because you can't access them; they're not getting through.

45

We all have our own personal mine full of these precious gems, but often their way is blocked. BBM gives you the mechanism to break through the barriers, to reach these skills, to develop them, and to transform your life.

Only within yourself exists that reality for which you long

HERMAN HESSE

Each barrier blocks certain skills, holding within it this potential; in recognition of this, the skills are known by the barrier that blocks them, such as the backward focus skills.

Summary

This chapter has outlined the four stages of the BBM process EAST. The first stage is explore, when you gain an overview of each focus, understanding how its dominant influence steals attention and causes it to become a barrier. The next stage is assess, when you learn how to recognise the inhibitors that alert you to the presence of a barrier. Shift is the third stage where you find the best counteracting approaches to remove a barrier, by shifting attention back into the balance of forward focus. The final stage is about the soft skills you're able to access when you break through a barrier, and how this will transform your life.

Autobiography In Five Short Chapters

by Portia Nelson

I
I walk down the street.
There is a deep hole in the sidewalk
I fall in.
I am lost ... I am helpless.
It isn't my fault.
It takes me forever to find a way out.

II
I walk down the same street.
There is a deep hole in the sidewalk.
I pretend I don't see it.
I fall in again.
I can't believe I am in the same place
but, it isn't my fault.
It still takes a long time to get out.

III
I walk down the same street.
There is a deep hole in the sidewalk.
I see it is there.
I still fall in ... it's a habit.
My eyes are open
I know where I am.
It is my fault.
I get out immediately.

IV
I walk down the same street.
There is a deep hole in the sidewalk.
I walk around it.

V
I walk down another street.

4 Backward Focus

Moving The Past Out Of Your Way

Explore Backward Focus

When Backward Focus becomes a barrier it's because our attention has been drawn by its **dominant influence: past**.

The past has many facets. Of course there's our own past, of which childhood is undoubtedly our most formative time, and the family our most defining experience. We've all grown up within some kind of family structure, even if the family was physically absent. We're part of a pre-existing network that drapes a particular role around us from infancy, and which we accept as normality. We construct our life view from this perspective, building the way we see ourselves as individuals and our place within our community. The role we're given as an infant can stay with us forever.

What was your family role? The favourite? Scapegoat? The shy one? The smart one? Tough guy? The pretty one? Loner? Clown? Naughty? The invisible one?

These roles are other people's interpretations of how we fit into their group; our role is conjured up from others' values and expectations…from the past. It may or may not match who we really are. Yet over time we're quite likely to adapt ourselves to fit the role…"if this is how I'm seen this is how I must be". Our early environment moulds our self-image and now, although we have no memory of that time, the role may still direct our sense of identity and loom large in our life.

> One gets large impressions in boyhood, sometimes,
> which he has to fight against all his life
>
> **MARK TWAIN**

Did you accept your role? Buck against it? Ignore it?

How true to the real you do you think your role was?

Few of us had an entirely secure, untroubled upbringing; some of us could spend a lifetime unravelling our early experiences, and many of us do. An in-depth unravelling can be valuable if those formative years contain damaging trauma, and a protracted period of backward focus may be called for in order to move beyond it. For most, just developing an awareness of how our family has defined us is hugely valuable. Without this we can unwittingly be locked into a way of being that's not true to who we really are. The key to moving on from this is to recognise where our true self diverges from the role we've adopted.

Understanding this gives us freedom to make choices, rather than being unconsciously driven by backward focus.

> Freedom is what you do
> with what's been done to you
>
> **JEAN-PAUL SARTRE**

Did your role in the family change over time—or is it the same now as when you were a child?

What's your relationship to that role today?

Backward focus also refers to how we fit into our broader society, how we're perceived in the context of our particular time and place; in other words, how the culture we're born into receives us, the affect that has on how we perceive ourselves, how that influences our life, how it has socialised us.

Some 'boxes' are ours from birth, and have little scope for change. We'll be categorised according to gender; age; ethnicity; religion; class; physical appearance; and so on.

Other boxes we get put into throughout our lives, according to factors such as education; marital status; career; children; financial status; and political affiliation.

All these boxes have weighty expectations attached to them. Packed like Russian dolls, each box has within it several more. What we believe about ourselves and our capabilities, our understanding of 'success', what we think we should have achieved and by what time in our lives, these are all largely defined by existing, external criteria; in effect, we're defined by someone else's past, rather than by our own experience of the present.

And the meaning of the boxes varies enormously according to context...for example, factors that influence the way our bodies are perceived include the era we live in (Who's beautiful, a rotund Rubens nymph or a super skinny model?), the current fashion (Men in tights?), the prevailing religion (Which bits of our body are most shameful?) and our culture (Exactly how much hair is respectable or attractive, and whereabouts is it desirable, removed, or forbidden?).

Once, not so long ago, we would all have been defined by those in our immediate neighbourhood. Now, in an age of global interconnectedness and mass communication, there's a new challenge. It's impossible for us to avoid a bombardment of societal assumptions, and the marketing ploys that feed on and into this, designed to provoke our dissatisfaction. Rather than feeling joy in riches we already possess, our discontent is stoked and our attention prodded into the backward focus direction of someone else's airbrushed reality.

Care about other people's opinion and you will be their prisoner

TAO TE CHING

For some this works. Perhaps they manage to ignore the boxes, fit into them OK, or get something out of them. But for many, backward focus isn't just a context framing their life but has become a barrier locking them within personal, social, or legal boundaries. Their horizons narrow, potential withers, and happiness dims.

Assess Backward Focus

Once we recognise backward focus, we can examine our life and see whether it is present. If backward focus is in balance with the other focuses, the past usefully informs our journey. If it's over-dominant, the past constrains us.

> *This above all: to thine own self be true*
> WILLIAM SHAKESPEARE

In the previous section we considered the influence of our family and up-bringing on our self-perception, in particular, the role we had in our family.

How deeply have you questioned your family role before?

Has your family role stayed with you?

If it has, are you happy with it?

If you're not happy with it, how does it limit you?

What role better suits you now?

We also considered the effects of society's backward focus boxes on us. Sometimes these boxes cause us to put the brakes on our own actions; for example, "I'm too old / stupid / short to achieve this", or "I'm not educated / rich / handsome enough to go there", or "Men / mothers / English people don't do that".

Do any of society's backward focus boxes limit yours actions and goals?

If so, which ones and how?

We might not even know that we've been put into a box and it's counted against us. Different cultures and sub-cultures have different kinds of 'class' systems. Some are widespread—such as gender, race, and disability; others may be more localised—accent, haircut, school, neighbourhood. All define and limit the individual. Anti-discrimination laws have recognised the prominent inequities, but many attitudes are determined and deeply ingrained; their response to criticism is to become covert, pushed underground, still lurking, but harder to recognise…in ourselves and others.

Do you believe that backward focus has caused other individuals to judge you

or limit your actions?

If so, which boxes have they put you in?

Do you feel that this is still happening in your life?

If so, how can you challenge it?

Which boxes do you tend to put people into?

How could this limit them?

Cultural, religious, and social doctrines give us codes to live by and a moral compass to help us navigate our life journey. However, they can also strictly define how we should act. Those who disobey the rules will be judged according to the backward focus lore of that particular group.

Are your actions limited by any of the doctrines you live within?

How do these beliefs or values hinder you?

Do you have to follow any rules that go against what your heart feels is right

for you?

If so, what are they?

There are numerous examples of backward focus group-think. To be accepted by a particular group, gang, team, club, cult, or society you must conform to a particular set of rules. In many circumstances rules are, of course, necessary and acceptable; in others, backward focus applies rigid restrictions on personal freedom, and severely punishes the disobedient.

> *Loyalty to petrified opinion*
> *never yet broke a chain*
> *or freed a human soul*
>
> **MARK TWAIN**

Have you ever been part of any such group?

Have you ever been excluded by any such group?

Recognising how the past has affected us gives us the ability to respond to it as we choose. We can learn from it, find creative ways to mitigate any negative effects, and make sure that whatever we carry with us is supporting our future.

Here are some thoughts for you to complete spontaneously:

If I change I might...

Taking a risk means...

I used to be...

All my ideas are...

Tradition represents...

I think mistakes are...

I worry that...

I'm glad I no longer...

My standards are...

In my daydreams I...

I see the past as...

I see the future as...

If I could I'd...

I look forward to...

I no longer need to be...

Being different is...

The past is never dead.

It's not even past.

All of us labor in webs spun long before we were born,

webs of heredity and environment,

of desire and consequence,

of history and eternity

WILLIAM FAULKNER

Shift Backward Focus

Each barrier has a counteracting approach that you apply to overcome it, shifting your attention to forward focus. To counteract the impact of backward focus use **self-referring approaches**. These give us the opportunity to recognise and develop our own opinions, thoughts, feelings, and identity, and to detach these from the dominating influence of others and the past.

It is a poor sort of memory
that only works backwards

LEWIS CARROLL

As with all counteracting approaches, there are numerous ways that you can apply them to your life, and how you do this will depend upon your unique circumstances.

Suggestions for self-referring approaches that you can practice while reading this book are set out below.

Journal

It's not essential to use a journal while reading *Barrier Breakers: Be Yourself Brilliantly!* However, it's a really effective way to get the most from the book, and to make the most profound shifts. If you choose to use one you can either use *The Journal* that accompanies this book, or you can create your own. Keep the journal and book together, so the journal can be to hand as you read. As well as using it for the exercises, jot down any thoughts you have as you go along; things you find funny, or frustrating; anything that doesn't make sense or that rings a big bell; a quote that resonates with you; a seemingly unrelated hunch or idea; a doodle; a dream you have; or a coincidence that happens. Document your experience of reading this book, to capture and develop your thoughts and ideas.

Set Your Priority

Consider your strengths and weaknesses. Write them down. Question any assumptions you've previously made about them; remember that you may have many pre-conceived notions about your capabilities. We can carry these with us from childhood, from our education, from past experiences. We can forget that we've changed, and what we once found beyond us is now easily within our grasp, if we allow it to be.

A key reason that adults tend to find it more difficult than children to learn something new is that adults are much harder on themselves. When you were very young you had no notion of how long any particular learning should take, so you just got on with being curious. You attached no particular value to outcome, so you were free to get absorbed in process. You didn't think of yourself in terms of being stupid, so you didn't get angry with yourself if you made a mistake. Things changed when others' expectations made you self-conscious, and the barriers started to build.

At first a childhood, limitless and free
Of any goals. Ah, sweet unconsciousness.
Then sudden terror, schoolrooms, slavery.
The plunge into temptation and deep loss
RAINER MARIA RILKE

Learn from the easy way you used to learn; assess yourself with a detached, affectionate, open mind, from the perspective of curiosity rather than of expectation and irritation.

How do your current strengths and weaknesses affect your life?

Some of your weaknesses will make little difference to you on a daily basis, and these you can put to one side. Others you may be able to overcome by delegating or hiring the necessary skills, so ignore these for now. Instead, identify a particular attitude or behaviour you have that's stopping you from doing something you'd love to do, or need to do—something that relates to the change you have in mind; this is your priority.

> *The most important choice you make is what you choose to make important*
>
> **MICHAEL NEILL**

Make a note of your priority, along with all the compelling reasons why you want to change it. Keep it in your awareness; carry it with you; put it through the BBM process. See how it changes by the time you've finished the book.

Catch 'n' Let Go

We've all experienced irritatingly infectious advertising slogans, or catchy jingles that we only heard subliminally, yet end up playing on a loop in our brains! Our memories are radars, picking up and storing masses of information, some from times long ago that we can't even remember, and mostly difficult to organise and recall efficiently. It's very easy for our thoughts to be infiltrated by an invasive backward focus thought. If we've heard something consistently throughout our life there's a good possibility we'll recall it as something we actually believe, particularly when the incoming messages are persistent and personal. However, when we become conscious of these backward focus thoughts we realise they don't originate with us, any more than the slogan or jingle. This awareness gives us the freedom to choose our thoughts for ourselves.

We are not animals.
We are not a product
of what has happened to us in our past.
We have the power of choice

STEPHEN COVEY

Start to notice if backward focus is controlling your thoughts. When you hear a thought that defines you, grab hold of it. Does its tone shame or encourage? Does it restrict you, or help you reach further? Could it have come from your earlier life, from someone else, or is it definitely the current you? Is it the way you wish to be? Does it sound like a prejudiced criticism or a reasonable judgment? Does it feel invasive or benign? Check that it's speaking your truth rather than being the limiting voice of backward focus.

To find yourself, think for yourself

SOCRATES

If it's an invasive backward focus thought, you want to reduce its control. Identify what you really think, rather than accepting what the thought delivers to you. Create your own thought—stated in the positive—that contradicts the invasive thought. Every time the invasive thought comes into your mind, calmly repeat your counteracting statement. Again, be sure this statement is in the positive. And be persistant!

> *Our life is what our thoughts make it*
> MARCUS AURELIUS ANTONINUS

BBM doesn't require you to turn your attention to the origins of your thoughts; BBM's purpose is to help you move your attention away from backward focus. In this process you devote you energy to chasing and catching the invasive thought, recognising that you don't own it, quietening it with the counteracting statement, and letting it go. The thought will undoubtedly continue to visit, and possibly be increasingly persistent for a while, especially if it's been a part of your life for a long time. But it will become less frequent as you get better at disregarding and dismissing it. And eventually it will get bored and go away.

Make a note of your regular backward focus thoughts as they arise. Create the counteracting statements and remember them.

When you finish reading this book, review these backward focus thoughts and see how their frequency and intensity has altered.

> *A mind that is stretched*
> *by a new experience*
> *can never go back to its old dimensions*
>
> OLIVER WENDELL HOLMES

New Experiences

Try the following new experiences over the next few days:

- Eat a food you've never tried, or one that you ate when you were a child and didn't like. Unless you really dislike it, try it twice to see how the taste changes the second time around.

- Have a new cultural experience…go to an exhibition, play, concert, or show that you'd never normally think of going to.

- Put on something that you'd not usually wear. Then go for a walk…

Make a note about what you did and how it felt.

Keep looking out for the opportunity to have new experiences, however small, and revisit things that you discounted in the past.

Transform Backward Focus

As you incorporate self-referring approaches into your life, you shift your attention towards forward focus. With this, you increasingly access and develop a range of soft skills that get blocked by backward focus—the **backward focus skills.**

Whenever you want to use BBM to support you through a specific change, backward focus is a good place to begin the process. Also, if you're looking to develop your leadership qualities or to become more adept at managing change generally, the backward focus skills are ones you'll want to develop.

> *Think wrongly, if you please,*
> *but in all cases think for yourself*
> DORIS LESSING

When you apply self-referring approaches, such as those in the previous section, you have opportunities to challenge invasive thinking patterns, and to recognise when these thoughts are out of alignment with your real feelings, damaging your well-being. You become more in tune with your own perspective, stepping outside your boxes, and questioning societal assumptions and expectations.

> *Things do not change; we change*
> HENRY DAVID THOREAU

Self-referring approaches increase your self-awareness and strengthen your self-perception. Catching your limiting thoughts, questioning their legitimacy, and counteracting them with your own opinions becomes habitual. This builds clarity and confidence in your own beliefs and opinions. You become more conscious of how you see yourself now and where you wish to go in future. This builds independent judgment, and self-reliance.

You ask yourself powerful questions to uncover whether your thoughts truly represent your beliefs, or whether backward focus has produced a barrier; in doing this, you may challenge things you've accepted or believed all your life. To question accepted thinking, particularly one's own, takes great courage.

Always the beautiful answer
who asks a more beautiful question
E E CUMMINGS

We construct our reality to make sense of the world as we find it, and to give ourselves a kind of security. We might build something that's not in our own best interest, but our mind hangs onto it because it's all we've got. At a rational level we might accept that change is needed. We also know that change is inevitable, even if we don't know what it will be or when it will happen. Despite this, we tend to get defensive about making changes, and especially if someone else is telling us to do it. So BBM helps us to:

- be in control of our own change

- be adaptable

- draw our own conclusions regarding our behaviour

- discover the advantages in change, rather than doing it to comply with someone else's expectations

- be responsible for our own path

- allow it to take as long as it takes.

We are constantly in a state of becoming

BOB DYLAN

To seek support and advice is valuable and at times essential, but BBM works from the starting point of trusting ourselves as individuals to determine our own change, rather than believing we need to look outside ourselves for others' opinion or validation. To learn, to grow, to be inquisitive and creative; these are all natural human instincts that we can draw on and in which we find pleasure. Make these a central part of your change process, and change will be pleasurable too.

Summary

So, in conclusion, self-referring approaches allow you remove the barrier of backward focus, and to access and develop your innate capacity for reflection and self-assessment, your ability to ask probing questions, and your independent judgment. The process encourages you to use your initiative, and hones your self-perception. This clarifies your personal vision, and provides the strength of purpose that fuels enlightened leadership of all kinds—whether you need this as a teacher, manager, parent, mentor, employer, or simply as an adult.

All's Well that Ends Well

Act 1 Scene 1

by Shakespeare

Our remedies oft in ourselves do lie

Which we ascribe to heaven; the fated sky

Gives us free scope; and only backward pulls

Our slow designs when we ourselves are dull.

How much I could do if I only tried.

5 Inward Focus
Getting Inside Out

Explore Inward Focus

When inward focus becomes a barrier it's because our attention has been drawn by its **dominant influence: self**

As with all the focuses, inward focus has many benefits—it's the focus we use when we're studying, reflecting, reading, practicing yoga…doing anything that engages us completely, to the exclusion of others.

However, if inward focus draws our attention too often and inappropriately, then it becomes a barrier. For example, as a musician you need a concentrated inward focus when you're practising your instrument. But imagine what would happen if inward focus was still in the driving seat when you went to rehearse with your group? Or as you're negotiating a contract? Or performing in front of an audience?

The barrier of inward focus doesn't just affect individuals. For example, it affects families—stacking up family secrets, blocking connection to the outside world, using messages such as "blood is thicker than water" to force compliance.

Inward focus is apparent in the many different types of communities that live within narrow boundaries marked by high fences—those that frown upon friendships with 'outsiders', specify suitable marriage partners, or only undertake business with people of their type.

An organisation affected by inward focus will resist new ideas, playing it safe, working with what it already has and already knows, only changing if change is forced upon it. In order to keep this status quo, the organisation expects its employees to tow the company line, and they in turn self-censor, knowing that bringing anything new to the table isn't to their advantage. Inward focus damages all communication channels, internal and external.

Inward focus may affect a particular level or department in an organisation. It's not uncommon for those at the top of a hierarchy to be afflicted by it, eliminating the empathy that's needed to understand those working at the coal face. This has various negative effects, including a reduction in workforce well-being, and increased stress levels, leading to demotivation and decline in productivity.

> *The most important single ingredient*
> *in the formula of success*
> *is knowing how to get along with people*
> **THEODORE ROOSEVELT**

An organisation may believe that inward focus is necessary to preserve its identity or brand. But many become so used to this way of being that they're blinkered to change happening all around them, realising too late that their offering is no longer worth preserving.

*Successful organisations will be those
who can do more than embrace change—
they will anticipate, identify and drive it*

MARY CHAPMAN

Institutions with inward focus become swaddled in their internal processes and politics, losing touch with those they were established to serve. Engrossed in their own issues, they treat the 'general public' as somehow different and less important than themselves, and their customers become an irritation. Increasingly habituated to their work, they're unable to feel compassion, and no longer empathise with even the most distressed clients.

Inward focus stretches out to affect countries, from restrictions instigated by autocratic regimes, to covert chauvinism found in the mass media of democracies. The impact of a society's inward focus has a profound impact on everyone.

But that's another discussion! Our concern here is with inward focus as it affects us on a personal level.

Assess Inward Focus

When we know how to recognise inward focus, we can assess our own life to see if Inward Focus is playing any part, and holding us back in any way.

When Inward Focus is in balance with the other focuses, we have a good sense of being ourselves while being connected to others. If it's over-dominant, our relationships will be blighted by poor communication and lack of understanding.

Inward focus has numerous manifestations, some of them seemingly contradictory. For example, it causes an exaggerated sense of entitlement, an "I know it all already, I'm fabulous, and I'm it" attitude. But as well as producing this loud, 'in-your-face' type of behaviour, inward focus is also behind shyness.

Shyness has a strange element of narcissism,
a belief that how we look, how we perform,
is truly important to other people

ANDRE DEBUS

Although perceived by some as a charming quality, and seen as an integral part of feminity in certain cultures, shyness is a crippling inhibitor of potential and distressing for the person suffering from it. Whatever brings on the shyness, it has its roots in self-consciousness; attention is so focused inward that it's impossible to extend out into the environment.

Does inward focus affect you in either of the ways described above?
Where do you encounter inward focus behaviour in others?

The barrier of inward focus isn't about being introvert or extravert; it's about attention being so drawn to the self that we're unable to engage fully with others.

Somebody is boring me...I think it's me
DYLAN THOMAS

Inward focus also makes it difficult for us to see long term, or to see the bigger picture. This means that we get caught up with things that provide immediate gratification. Inward focus blinds us to the impact our behaviour has on others, or on ourselves in the long term; these are too far outside our present selves to grasp, so they don't exist. Our feelings become trapped inside ourselves, limited only to how we feel in the moment...I kick you but I feel no pain, therefore there is none, other than the pain you're giving me by complaining; the cream cake is so real, the weight-gain just a concept.

Have you ever used the term 'addictive personality' to describe yourself?

Do you have to work hard at self-control in any area of your life?

Do people ever say you've hurt their feelings?

If so, what's your response?

When inward focus is dominating us, our priority is to maintain our sense of self. If anything tries to shake our reality we'll resist it. This will happen even if our reality is hurting us; someone with low self-esteem can be very sure of themselves, in that it will be almost impossible for somebody else to instil in them an awareness of their positive qualities.

Do you have any trait that you know is causing damage, but you can't let go of it?

Inward focus is essentially solipsistic; it causes us to think that only 'I' am of any consequence. From shyness, through the arrogance of entitlement, to narcissism, there are many disparate branches springing from the root of inward focus. It cuts off others' influence or perspective, so it grows without allowing anything outside itself to play a part in its direction. It will do this even if the decision it reaches as a result defies logic, or isn't in anyone's best interest. Because of this incongruity, it can be difficult for those coming into contact with inward focus to recognise or understand it.

It doesn't necessarily have a malign intent, but because inward focus doesn't have any sense of others as separate entities, only as satellites to 'planet me', it can inflict great damage to those around it.

The best way to keep a prisoner from escaping is to make sure he never knows he's in prison

DOSTOEVSKY

Is there anyone in your life who you think may have inward focus that's affecting you?

Do you think your inward focus could be a barrier for anyone else in your life?

Paradoxically, when the self is drawing all our attention we're unlikely to be acting in ways that support us in the long run. We're invariably in many and various relationships, and for them to be successful we need to have a flow of communication with them. Inward focus blocks this flow; the barrier closes off communication channels. It doesn't understand compromise, can't listen to another point of view, and only shares on its own terms.

Any relationship affected by inward focus becomes frustrated by the lack of adaptability and balance. This behaviour causes dysfunctional communication in numerous ways—from a lack of consideration of another's schedule, or an inability to negotiate effectively, to not being able to hear what a child is really saying, or being unsympathetic to a friend in need, through to various damaging forms of manipulation and control.

Does anyone ever say they don't feel that you're listening to them?

Which do you do more of–ask questions or give answers?

Are you more of a talker or a listener?

Do you tend to interrupt people?

Here are some thoughts for you to complete spontaneously:

I connect to others by...

I generate positive energy through...

Sharing ideas means...

I contribute by...

When I listen to others I...

When I express my opinions I...

A conversation is...

When someone points out a mistake I've made I...

If someone asks for my opinion I'm...

One of my habitual words is...

If I interrupt someone...

Talking in public is...

Shift Inward Focus

To counteract the impact of inward focus use **empathic approaches.** Look for opportunities to turn your attention towards others, to understand their circumstances, consider things from their perspective, and respond productively to them. The empathic approaches you choose and how you apply them will depend on your own situation.

Suggestions for some empathic approaches that you can use while reading this book are set out below.

Word Play

The power of words is colossal. The saying "sticks and stones can break my bones but words can never harm me" is wrong; the words we choose, the way we say them, plus our non-verbal communication through facial expression and body language are a potent combination and a potentially lethal concoction.

As a warm-up, say each of the following sentences, emphasising the word indicated. Consider how the emphasis changes the meaning. Choose from the 'Meanings' list to link each sentence to the meaning produced by each emphasis. The first one is done for you:

	Sentence		Meanings
1	*I* never said she bit my dog		She bit something else of mine
2	I *never* said she bit my dog		She bit someone else's dog
3	I never *said* she bit my dog	1	~~Someone else said it~~
4	I never said *she* bit my dog		I only thought it
5	I never said she *bit* my dog		It wasn't her that bit it
6	I never said she bit *my* dog		I wouldn't say such a thing
7	I never said she bit my *dog*		She did something else to it

> *Words are, of course,*
> *the most powerful drug used by mankind*
>
> RUDYARD KIPLING

The words you choose

Notice the habitual words you use. Do you:

- exaggerate with dramatic, over-the-top language?

- use a lot of judgemental words like 'should' or 'ought'?

- often include dogmatic words such as 'always', or 'never'?

- use negative language, perhaps saying you 'hate' things?

- negate yourself or others?

- use sarcasm a lot?

- have habitual phrases, 'tics' that could distract a listener and interrupt your message?

The way you say them

Listen to the tone of your voice. If you were the listener what would you hear? Record yourself if you're not sure. Is it a pleasant sound? Is it whiny? Aggressive? Or monotone? Are you conveying enthusiasm or boredom?

Your non-verbal communication

Think about whether your facial expression and body language gets your message across effectively. Do they match what you're saying, or does the combination produce a mixed message? If you saw and heard yourself, what would you think?

Your intended meaning

To convey our intended meaning we need to consider what we're communicating in these three ways at any one time: the words we choose, the way we say them, and our non-verbal communication. Practise becoming aware of this. Observe yourself and others. Find opportunities to play around with the way you communicate. See how you can produce different responses.

> *Words have the power*
> *to both destroy and heal.*
> *When words are both true and kind,*
> *they can change our world*
>
> BUDDHA

Words As Weapons

Words are tools of control when coming from the mouths of manipulators. And manipulators can be found in all shapes and sizes. Those who are expert at this form of inward focus do not need a lesson in its effectiveness; those who don't do it are usually completely unaware that it's being done to them, and fall unwittingly under its spell.

Verbal abuse is most destructive when it's covert; it's much harder to challenge anything when it's hidden, and this form of inward focus is one of the most duplicitous barriers.

*A blow with a word
strikes deeper
than a blow with a sword*
ROBERT BURTON

Learn about how words are used by manipulators. Find out about the various techniques that might be used against you or others. *The Verbally Abusive Relationship* by Patricia Evans[1] details many methods of verbal control, including withholding; discounting; verbal abuse disguised as a joke; accusing and blaming; judging and criticizing; trivializing; undermining; threatening; name calling. Anyone can sometimes inadvertently use this kind of language—manipulators use it consistently and knowingly.

Learn how to deflect these techniques.

Practise.

Listen out for instances of these techniques in action.

Recognise them if you use them yourself, and remove them from your vocabulary.

---

1. Evans, P. (1996). *The Verbally Abusive Relationship: how to recognise it and respond.* Adams Media.

Good Listening

Listening to someone makes the speaker feel valued and respected. It's also the best way for the listener to learn. So 'good' listening is a win-win practice, and it's a natural ability we all have. We can remind ourselves of how to do it just by considering how we like to be listened to. Given that good listening is so beneficial to listener and speaker, and makes such a positive difference to personal and work relationships, it's strange that good listening isn't more common.

> *If we were supposed to talk more than we listen, we would have two mouths and one ear*
>
> **MARK TWAIN**

Inward focus blocks good listening, making it impossible for the listener to disengage themselves enough from themselves to have any attention left over for another—everything they hear is directed through their own filter, distorted by their internal chatter.

Practise good listening and notice the difference it makes to your relationships. First, listen to someone and give your attention entirely to them. Notice which thoughts come up to distract your attention; let the thoughts go and refocus your attention on the speaker. Initially you could try this with someone you don't have to respond to—someone on radio or TV, a lecturer, someone else in a large group.

Make a note of which of your internal thoughts distracted you while you were listening. Did you...

- daydream?

- want to butt in?

- mind read what the speaker was really thinking?

- plan what you wanted to say to them?

- get reminded of something in your own life, and think about that?

- compare yourself to the speaker?

- think about what the speaker looked like?

Once you've mastered focusing your attention, and have taken control away from inward focus, try it in a one-to-one conversation. What happened?

- Were you genuinely engaged with what the speaker was saying?

- Did you interrupt them?

- How long was it before your mind wandered?

- Could you manage to refrain from giving unsolicited advice?

- Did you resist referring the conversation back to yourself before the speaker completed their train of thought?

- If there was silence, were you comfortable letting it be for a few moments, so thoughts could settle?

Silence is a source of great strength

LAO TZU

When you're in conversation also be aware of your body language, and what that communicates. Are you facing the speaker, maintaining regular eye contact, and responding appropriately? If you're genuinely interested in what someone is saying, your body language will naturally reflect this, so no conscious effort is necessary. However, it's worth taking stock in case you've got any distracting habits. Inward focus has canny ways of getting the attention back to you…hair twiddling, pen clicking, change rattling and so on!

Keep finding opportunities to practise good listening. Note how it affects the conversations at the time, and your relationships more broadly. It's a very useful technique to use when you're meeting new people and networking—you'll enjoy the occasion much more, and research shows that you'll get the bonus of being considered a great communicator.

Let a fool hold his tongue
and he will pass for a sage

PUBLILIUS SYRUS

Reaching Out

Do the following activities over the next few days:

- Introduce yourself to someone and find out about them.

- Offer to do something for someone unexpectedly.

- Express appreciation to someone who's helped you.

- Give someone a small gift for no reason; don't tell anyone else about it.

- Compliment someone you don't know well.

How did it feel?

Is this similar to your normal behaviour or quite out of character?

Record your thoughts.

Keep looking for opportunities to reach out and do 'small things'.

> We cannot do great things on this earth.
> We can only do small things
> with great love
>
> MOTHER THERESA

Transform Inward Focus

As you incorporate more empathic approaches into your life, you shift towards forward focus. With this, you increasingly access and develop a range of soft skills that inward focus was blocking—the **inward focus skills**. These are the skills that allow you to communicate effectively in relationships of all kinds.

When you apply empathic approaches, such as those discussed in the previous section, you have opportunities to identify whether inward focus is blocking your communication channels, to locate where the barrier is, to recognise whether it originates with you or someone else, and to determine how best to remove it.

Empathic approaches enhance communication, improving all your interpersonal interactions, and enabling you to be more in tune with the way that words, paralanguage (tone of voice etc.) and body language are used, both to achieve positive outcomes, and for reasons of control.

Improving your listening skills through empathic approaches gives you the ability to shift your attention away from yourself, and be genuinely interested in and curious about others. By listening attentively and asking questions for clarification, you learn more than if you were doing all the talking; you're perceived as having good communication skills; you enjoy yourself more because you won't be itching to interrupt people with 'me' talk; and you'll relax because you won't need to be the centre of attention.

*The way you overcome shyness
is to become so wrapped up in something
that you forget to be afraid*

CLAUDIA LADY BIRD JOHNSON

Negotiation requires us to know how we can meet the needs of another, and what they're prepared to offer in return. Being able to understand someone's position allows you to take the best stance from which to negotiate the most desirable outcome. An empathic approach works whoever you're negotiating with—a client, a partner, or a child. Your terms may be very demanding, but if you can align them to the other's position you're more likely to get a satisfactory result.

*If there is any one secret of success,
it lies in the ability
to get the other person's point of view*

HENRY FORD

Another skill that you'll access through empathic approaches is the ability to work well in a team. Teams generally come together based on what members do. Whether they'll get on as individuals is usually last on the list of concerns; however, many teams fall apart, and their projects flounder, because of 'people problems' and personal clashes. With an empathic approach you reduce this likelihood. If you understand another's position you can be more aware and acceptant of differences, and work with them more readily; you'll also foresee potential problems, diffusing them before they become engrained. You achieve this primarily by listening objectively and hearing what people are really saying rather than projecting your own agenda onto them. Once you know someone's concerns and expectations, you're far better equipped to communicate in ways that respond directly to these, reducing tensions and promoting unity.

> *The leaders who work most effectively,*
> *never say "I."*
> *They think "we"; they think "team"*
>
> PETER DRUCKER

We all need to be able to speak in front of others at some time, yet fear of public speaking is said to be greater for many than the fear of dying! However, too often it's the audience who's put at risk of dying through boredom…have you ever watched a presentation and wondered whether the presenter would have enjoyed being their own audience member?

As a presenter you can rarely tailor a presentation to suit each individual audience member, but you can still use an empathic approach to benefit everyone. Again, the key is to shift away from inward focus, and put your attention onto those you'll be speaking to. Unlike a performance, where the aim is to offer yourself to an audience, a presentation's purpose is to offer information. Rather than delivering in the way that suits you, ask what's the best approach to take for your audience? What kind of language will they understand best? How will you adapt your message to be heard by engineers, artists, academics, 6-year-olds, wedding guests or investors? Put yourself into their shoes, and design the presentation from this stance. The result will be relevant, direct, and engaging; you'll get your point across, and your audience will stay awake. As a bonus, shifting inward focus by putting an audience first means you stop being self-absorbed, which reduces nerves.

Summary

In conclusion, using empathic approaches allows you to remove the barrier of inward focus, and to access and develop your innate capacity for empathic communication with others. The process enables you to deepen your understanding of another's position, which improves your social interaction in all situations. As your verbal communication and listening skills develop, you become more attuned to the way words are used, from the most positive reasons through to forms of control.

Removing inward focus means you have more of yourself to give, and in return achieve better outcomes for yourself. Shifting focus away from self and onto others makes more sense of all interpersonal activities. By increasing your understanding and acceptance of the inevitable differences between people, you reduce your own irritation that they're not conforming to your perspective, and instead can put your energy into solutions. This makes you a more adept negotiator, a valuable team member, and someone who inspires as well as informs. Empathic approaches generate well-being, yours and others.

The Power of Words

by Letitia Elizabeth Landon

'Tis a strange mystery, the power of words!

Life is in them, and death. A word can send

The crimson colour hurrying to the cheek.

Hurrying with many meanings; or can turn

The current cold and deadly to the heart.

Anger and fear are in them; grief and joy

Are on their sound; yet slight, impalpable:--

A word is but a breath of passing air.

6 Downward Focus

Shining A Light On The Shadow

Explore Downward Focus

When downward focus becomes a barrier it's because our attention has been drawn by its **dominant influence: shadow**

> *Everyone carries a shadow,*
> *and the less it is embodied*
> *in the individual's conscious life,*
> *the blacker and denser it is*
>
> CARL JUNG

The psychiatrist Carl Jung used the term 'shadow' to describe the dark side of the psyche, our unconscious. In BBM, shadow has a similar meaning, but rather than being a psychological term, here it refers more generally to the unacknowledged, hidden side of a person, group, organisation, or any situation. If shadow draws attention and directs behaviour, then downward focus becomes a barrier, rather than being part of a balanced forward focus.

Ill-health, bereavement, relationship problems, financial difficulties, addictions…there are many reasons why an underlying issue can affect everything in someone's life. Occasionally the resulting emotions, such as acute grief, need to become the driving force, and downward focus must take precedence for a time, so the issue can be dealt with and moved beyond. But more often, a problem doesn't demand such intense attention, it just seeks recognition. In that way we assimilate it, rather than allowing it to control us covertly, through actions and emotions that invariably don't serve us well.

> *Under all that we think,*
> *lives all we believe,*
> *like the ultimate veil of our spirits*
>
> ANTONIO MACHADO

Downward focus can have many effects on us, depending on the particular shadow we're dealing with. Perhaps the pupil who's constantly disruptive in class is coping in their own way with a confusing family situation; or a colleague whose work has become lacklustre may be feeling trapped in a loveless marriage. Certain life events are common to us all and are therefore more easily recognised and accepted. But when the shadow is darker, clouded with shame, embarrassment, confusion, fear, or other such emotions, then it's more obscure and becomes harder for us to identify in ourselves or others.

Most often downward focus isn't a consequence of current events but of circumstances we may no longer remember, or have hidden from ourselves in order to cope. It may be due to our inability to acknowledge something that we think of as undesirable in ourselves, but can equally be caused by our inability to accept what someone else has done to us. As children we erroneously take on the blame for something, rather than believe ill of a parent, or someone we trust. Their downward focus produces ours, and we may then unwittingly live our life affected by our childish interpretation, tying ourselves up in ever more knots, rather than untangling ourselves from someone else's actions.

> *Those who cannot remember the past are condemned to repeat it*
> **GEORGE SANTAYANA**

While downward focus produces self-defeating emotions, the behaviours don't necessarily appear destructive. It's easier to recognise, for example, aggressive anger as being undesirable, but being too 'nice' can also be damaging, causing us to lack directness and tell white lies; it can make us try to reason with irrational people, or take on too much as we're unable to say no, and then become resentful. 'People-pleasers', along with those who avoid confrontation, or who need to maintain a particular image of themselves, will bewilder others by agreeing to one course of action with apparent enthusiasm, only to then take a quite different route that's more in line with their subconscious feelings.

This divergence between what someone says and what they do is just one example of downward focus causing chaos and confusion. Another is the impact of suppressed emotion, such as anger; if someone has anger bubbling beneath the surface they'll seem pleasant, until the anger erupts unpredictably, damaging all around it. When the anger subsides, and a calm demeanour returns, it's hard for those who were in the way of the fallout to reconcile themselves to what happened, and those who weren't witness to it may disbelieve it happened at all. Anyone who uses up energy by suppressing and then unleashing their emotions in this way, not only damages those around them, but also their own health and well-being.

Recognising downward focus is the first step to eliminating it as a barrier in ourselves, and dealing with it constructively when we encounter it in others. Because of the 'smoke and mirrors' nature of the barrier, we often have to rely on our gut feelings to recognise its presence. It may show up as our own seemingly irrational stress, or inexplicable procrastination about something we thought we wanted; we may suffer from terrible headaches or nausea doing what seems to others to be the perfect job; we may feel unease around someone who on paper we should like, or regularly feel pessimistic after spending time with a certain friend. If we don't pay attention to these messages then downward focus will continue to drive our behaviour, our bodies will send increasingly serious warnings about our 'dis-ease', and our lives will always be lived in the shadow.

> The truth will set you free.
> But first, it will piss you off
> **GLORIA STEINEM**

However, the more we respect our intuition, and develop our ability to connect with our own deeper wisdom, the more we'll recognise downward focus, finding ways to avoid it when it's coming from others, and to transform it in ourselves.

Just as downward focus afflicts individuals, it also damages the collective consciousness of groups, organisations, even countries. We all know of leaders who have galvanised entire nations of previously law-abiding citizens into acts of cruelty, manipulated as one into downward focus, their basest desires flipped into the accepted behaviour.

In organisations, downward focus is usually less extreme, but always covert. Whatever lies at its root, and whatever form it takes in any particular organisation, downward focus produces a toxic undercurrent that insinuates its way into every-thing, generating an atmosphere of anxiety and uncertainty. This climate doesn't tolerate failure, making everyone risk-averse, increasing their stress and reducing their creativity.

There are many examples of downward focus in even the most ostensibly pious organisations; there are well-known cases of religious bodies, education and health-care establishments, financial institutions and charities having been affected. The organisation's image to the outside world betrays nothing, its mask of respect-ability concealing internal issues that destroy not merely its effectiveness, but the well-being of its people, a malaise eroding potential and gnawing away at the spirit. This environment is a breeding ground for internal politics and power play, and it's here that bullying, a major cause of workplace stress, is completely at home. Everyone in the organisation is aware of a dark underbelly of shameful behaviour, but silence becomes the culture, and maintaining a pristine image the priority.

Company transformation must begin
with shifts that take place inside human beings

JUDITH E. GLASER

Downward focus holds the reins of any situation by forcing some kind of silence. If anyone dares to step out of the shadow and speak the truth, they risk being subjected to disbelief and ridicule. Downward focus is not only the most covert of the barriers, but also the most coercive.

> No person is your friend
> who demands your silence,
> or denies your right to grow
>
> ALICE WALKER

Assess Downward Focus

Being able to recognise downward focus enables us to assess our life to see if this barrier is affecting it in any way. The secretive nature of downward focus makes it the hardest of the barriers to identify, but we know it's in balance with the other focuses when we don't suffer from destructive behaviour patterns, or harmful emotions—ours or others'; when we're open to acknowledging our mistakes and examining problems as they arise; when we accept ourselves, warts and all; when we don't accept ill treatment by others. If downward focus is dominating us we'll have a sense that there's something holding us back, an unknown force that causes us to sabotage ourselves or hurt others; a shadow cast over all areas of our life.

Do you ever act in ways that self-sabotage?

If so, what do you do?

How does it affect your relationships?

Does it affect your work?

The shadow is, by its very nature, our blind side; an aspect of ourselves or someone else that we can't see, although we may well sense it. However, a shadow dissolves to nothing when we shine a light onto it, and this is what we do when we assess a situation for downward focus.

When do you think it's OK to tell a little white lie?

Do you find yourself doing it often?

Do you ever do it to yourself?

How do you feel about this?

The word 'personality' comes from the Latin 'persona' meaning 'mask'. We all have masks that we wear for different occasions; the 'you' on holiday is no doubt quite different from the 'you' at work. However, downward focus makes us concerned not just with how others perceive us, but with how we perceive ourselves.

> The persona is that which in reality
> one is not,
> but which oneself as well as others
> think one is
>
> CARL JUNG

Downward focus makes it crucial for us to maintain our illusion of who we are, and we expect others to reflect this back to us; others become our mirror. They let us know that our illusion is being successful, and if they don't reflect us back as we expect, we feel wronged and are likely to blame them, our 'mirror'.

In extreme cases, downward focus produces personality disorders and abusive behaviour, where an abuser is unable to take responsibility for their actions, believing as they do that their mask is reality. They blame their victim for making them act in ways that are out of character with their illusion of themselves. In this twisted mirror, the victim's self-perception is distorted not only by the action that's been perpetrated against them, but also by the blame for it. Of all the barriers, downward focus has the most devastating effect on those who come into contact with it.

> Selfishness is not living as one wishes to live;
> it is asking others to live as one wishes to live
> OSCAR WILDE

Even in less extreme situations, downward focus insists that we keep up appearances. If we're affected by it we can become blind to behaviours that are not only inconsiderate but seem illogical.

Do you ever agree to do something, and then act resentfully when you do it?
Do you ever tell a lie, saying it'll save someone's feelings—but knowing they'll find out the truth, plus they'll know you lied to them?

Downward focus won't help us find joy in our life—we're much too busy taking care of it to have time for that. It requires so much energy that we have little to spare. Planning in a calm and reasoned way isn't easy when downward focus keeps interrupting us with the voice of doubt and deception. In fact, the best thing to do is nothing at all. This will be the case whether the downward focus is ours, or we're in an environment that's governed by it: at home, at work, wherever. Among the catalogue of life-damaging effects caused by downward focus you'll find uncertainty and insecurity, which lead to procrastination and inertia.

> *To avoid criticism,*
> *do nothing,*
> *say nothing,*
> *be nothing*
>
> **ELBERT HUBBARD**

How does your inner voice talk to you? Is it encouraging or derogatory?

Do you worry a lot?

What's your favourite excuse for putting off doing something?

How often do you use it?

While doing nothing is the most obvious solution for avoiding risk, it's rarely an option. So, if downward focus is directing us we'll be uncomfortable and anxious whatever we do, primarily because we fear making mistakes. Our mask may exude confidence, but our task will be fraught and tense. We need our defences to be ready in case things go wrong, because our underlying fears make us very vulnerable to criticism. We can't stand failure; our default response to failure in ourselves is to transfer the blame elsewhere if we can.

Would you call yourself a perfectionist?

Would you prefer to take responsibility for a mistake you've made, or to lay the blame elsewhere?

Even if a problem is of our making, accepting responsibility for it opens us up to reprisal, so blaming someone or something else is the default position for downward focus. It forces us to devote a great deal of energy to minimising risk and to covering our backs. Rather than just getting on with things and enjoying life, downward focus confines us to the shadows, weighed down with the baggage of our hidden agenda.

If homo sapiens
was a species
with more courage,
we would identify
the demons
that frighten us,
confront them
and destroy them.
But it often seems easier
to hide

ROGER MAVITY

Here are some thoughts for you to complete spontaneously:

If I had no fear I'd be...

I'm motivated by...

I'm irritated by...

Jealous people are...

It makes me laugh when...

I feel strong if...

When I'm full of doubt I...

If someone treats me badly I...

Life is...

When others are more successful than me I feel...

If someone frustrates me I...

I feel connected to...

I feel rejected when...

In order to feel successful I must...

Shift Downward Focus

To counteract the impact of downward focus use **trust approaches**. These allow us to recognise and deepen our connection to our inner wisdom, to identify and free ourselves from limiting emotions, and to protect ourselves from 'emotional vampires'. There are many ways you can apply trust approaches in your life—you'll find the best ones for you.

Trust has several components and many interpretations. We most commonly associate it with our relationships, such as trust between partners, or in a business context. We ask ourselves whether another person has our best interests at heart. Do we believe what they tell us? Can we rely on them to keep their word?

But how often do we ask whether we trust ourselves? In fact, we're given many reasons not to trust ourselves. Every area of life is now scrutinised and monitored by 'experts', usually with the aim of getting us to buy something, or buy into someone. We're overwhelmed by information, choices, desirable products, perfect images. We're led to doubt our ability to do the most basic human activities adequately—to have a relationship, to be attractive, to be decent parents, to eat properly, to decorate our homes, even to be happy. There's an expert for every occasion. And we give them the right to label us, persuaded that they know who we are better than we do; they know which 'type' or 'style' we slot into, how we should work, live, learn, love, and how we can best be fixed.

In BBM, the barriers are not 'people labels', and trust approaches are about trusting yourself. People are pure potential. We all have an infinite capacity within us, far more than we could ever imagine. Barriers block our ability to access that capacity. Defining the barriers makes sense, because they're a theoretical construct. But to consistently define ourselves or anyone else denies the scope of human potential and limits our horizons.

> *As soon as you trust yourself*
> *you will know how to live*
>
> GOETHE

When you trust yourself you don't necessarily come up smelling of roses! Self-trust isn't born of a narcissistic blindness, but an eyes wide-open, persistently honest self-assessment. The more you identify and take responsibility for your emotions, motivations, thoughts, and actions, the more you'll be in charge of them. This self-awareness brings about self-acceptance, where you care about yourself, relishing the fabulousness and recognising the foibles.

When you accept yourself, you want to grow and change in ways that are meaningful to you, not in ways prescribed by an expert. When you trust your intuition, you know what's right for you, you move further towards solutions that bring you peace, and you're able to hear your inner voice warning you about someone or something that's liable to disrupt this simple intention.

> *Nothing can bring you peace but yourself*
> RALPH WALDO EMERSON

Your shadow side, once acknowledged, is the source of great inner wisdom, and trust approaches help you bring it to light.

Suggestions for some trust approaches that you can use while reading this book are set out below.

Under Words

When we looked at shifting inward focus, one of the suggested empathic approaches was 'Word Play' (page 77). 'Under Words' builds on that approach, so you might want to remind yourself of 'Word Play' to prepare for this exercise.

When you applied 'Word Play', you listened closely to what words were used by a speaker, and noticed the way they were delivered, including the tone of voice and body language. Now take this one step further. The next time someone's talking with you, be aware of how you feel physically. Rather than just responding intellectually, listen to what your body tells you.

What did your body say?

Were you relaxed or tense?

Did you feel connected to the person, or did you feel yourself shrink away?

Dids your physical response match up with what was being said?

Keep finding opportunities to check in with your physical responses; the body doesn't lie.

> I never get the accountants in
> before I start up a business.
> It's done on gut feeling
>
> RICHARD BRANSON

Sweet Talk

When we looked at counteracting approaches for backward focus, one of the suggestions was 'Catch 'n' Let Go' (page 60); 'Sweet Talk' builds on this technique.

We need to listen to what we say to ourselves habitually, and be sure that our inner voice can work in our best interest. All too often we have an invasive downward focus voice reverberating around our heads, filling our mental space with destructive chatter—some say it's as much as 90 per cent of our thoughts. This trust approach is about replacing the negative affirmations that downward focus chooses for you, with positive affirmations that you choose for yourself. This removes the invasive downward focus thoughts, clearing space for you to hear your own inner voice.

Positive affirmations are short, powerful statements that replace negative subconscious thoughts and build positive internal dialogue. In BBM these are used to counteract the downward focus thoughts that we recognise as limiting us and that we wish to move away from.

There are three key points to remember when creating positive affirmations. Make them:

1.   Positive—what you intend to have, not what you don't want

2.   Present—not in the future, or that's where it will always be

3.   Personal—it's not about changing or influencing others

Some examples of simple positive affirmations are:

•   I can handle whatever happens

•   I trust and believe in myself

•   I move beyond old limitations

Be aware of your self-defeating thoughts, as in 'Catch 'n' Let Go'; however, rather than creating a counteracting statement to use when a specific thought arises, now create positive affirmations to use at any time. Write them down; remember them. Repeat them to yourself as often as you like; for example, you can use them during meditation, when exercising, or to calm yourself in any difficult situation.

You'll probably sense initial resistance to some of the affirmations, and all the more so the further they are from your current reality—it'll feel like you're telling a big lie! But keep using them, apply passion to them, and you'll gradually shift downward focus. It takes persistence because the negative chatter has probably had free rein in your life until now, and downward focus doesn't give up without a fight. However, with practice you'll take charge of your habitual thoughts, and this is guaranteed to bring about major beneficial changes in your life.

Man is made by his belief.
As he believes, so he is

BHAGAVAD GITA

Stand Up To The Bully

Bullies use physical or psychological force to demean and demoralise someone else, to control them. Bullies turn up in many guises: in the classroom, the boardroom, at home, on sports teams, in cyberspace. Their actions can be extremely obvious, or confusingly covert. Consider where bullies might be in action in your life.

Does anyone pop into your head?

Is there any possibility that you bully somebody else in any way?

If you feel there's any bullying behaviour in your life this is an opportunity to look at it, to identify what you feel about it, and to decide what you can do to address it.

Have you been bullied? If you have, how did you deal with it?

Is it part of a pattern in your life?

> *Whilst accidents*
> *and assaults*
> *injure and kill people*
> *quickly and spectacularly,*
> *bullying,*
> *and consequent*
> *prolonged*
> *negative stress,*
> *injure and kill people*
> *slowly*
> *and secretively.*
> *The outcome, though,*
> *is the same*
>
> TIM FIELD

There's now a body of evidence to show how much bullying costs all of us, including bullies. Children who are bullies become aggressive adults with poor interpersonal skills, causing misery for themselves and others throughout their lives.

This week, take the following simple but powerful actions. You'll produce a ripple of long-term, positive impact:

- If you have school-age children in your life, do you know if their school is a bully-free zone? Find out if it has an anti-bullying programme.

- What about other people you know? Ask them whether they've ever been bullied. At home? At work? Online? Encourage them to talk about their experience of bullying.

- A sizeable proportion of the workforce can't work, due to stress caused by bullying in the workplace. The cost of bullying to UK industry and taxpayers is estimated to be at least £12 billion annually. If you work for an organisation, find out about its policy on bullying.

- Around 200 million children and youth globally are being bullied by their peers. Find out about this statistic. See if you can do one thing to change it, however small.

Goals

Write down three of your current key goals.

- Choose a mixture of long-term ones ("to go back to college and get a degree") and less ambitious ones ("to have a healthier diet").

- Relate at least one to the priority that you're taking through the book, from 'Set Your Priority' (page 58).

- Make sure the goals are achievable and not dependent on things outside your control.

- Turn these goals into positive affirmations, such as, "I'm now studying for the degree of my choice", and "I enjoy eating five portions of fruit and vegetables a day".

Write each of these affirmations on a postcard and put them where you'll see them several times a day. That's all you need to do for now.

This action will keep these goals in your mind, allowing your subconscious to mull them over.

You could put the cards on the fridge door, or the bathroom mirror. However, if you want to be more private, put them in your wallet, or diary—it's wise to do this if you have any sense that someone else might undermine what you're doing.

You may find yourself achieving the simpler goals naturally, without any effort. Unless there's a pressing deadline, let the more ambitious, long-term goals develop through imagination, intuition, coincidence and dreams, to clarify them, and to make sure you really want them. This process will build momentum, and motivate you to take action. So, for now, actively use your subconscious, and harness the creative energy of your shadow side.

Transform Downward Focus

As you use more trust approaches in your life you'll shift towards forward focus. With this, you increasingly access and develop a range of soft skills that get blocked by downward focus—the **downward focus skills**.

Downward focus skills build self-awareness, self-acceptance, and well-being. If downward focus is a barrier in any situation it's impossible for true confidence to also be present. Downward focus needs control over others to feel powerful, or even to have a sense of 'self'. It can never be satisfied in this quest, because there'll always be someone else it needs to conquer. It's an all-consuming, never-ending task.

Trust approaches release you from this endless striving. Instead of masking your shadow, you move towards a compassionate awareness of who you are now, and build your intention of the future. You cultivate a calm self-acceptance that releases personal power and genuine inner confidence.

110

Having self-confidence allows you to be assertive with others. This is the opposite of the aggression that downward focus uses to dictate what others must do; rather, this is knowing what you need to do, being able to state it calmly and clearly, respecting yourself.

Respect is love in plain clothes
FRANKIE BYRNE

This assertiveness is also about recognising when downward focus is present in your life, maybe in the form of others' controlling behaviour—it's about seeing it for what it is, and being able to move away from it. For many victims of downward focus, life stands still. They're so involved in dealing with the mayhem it causes that they're almost mesmerised, drained of energy and unable to move forward. Only once they've escaped the situation can they recognise what happened, describing the experience as like sinking in quicksand, or being a puppet, or treading water. Developing assertiveness helps to build the inner resources needed to move away from these situations.

*The last of the human freedoms
is to choose one's attitude
in any given set of circumstances*

VICTOR FRANKL

As well as deflecting negative behaviour, the assertiveness brought about by trust approaches allows you to promote yourself to others by being who you genuinely are, rather than by selling a hollow image, a mask. You don't need to put others down, or negate those you think are more successful than you are, in order to feel OK about yourself. Your self-assurance enables you to put yourself forward on your own merit and trusting yourself releases you from seeking others' approval.

Free from downward focus, and armed with inner confidence, your energy and enthusiasm can grow. No longer drained by the demands of downward focus, you can put all that extra energy into getting where you want to go. Instead of battling just to stay afloat, you can begin to move ahead, and this builds motivation as you see the changes happen. When you use up all your energy staying emotionally in one place it's hard to be optimistic; once that same energy produces results that you like, your motivation kicks into action. To grow and learn and change is natural human behaviour—in this we find joy. To remain the same is to stagnate, to atrophy.

As you develop self-awareness you're better able to interact with others. You no longer need to be defensive; you can listen to others' opinions without being on your guard, and can offer your opinion without any hidden agenda poisoning it. You can be given instructions by someone else without reacting as though they're controlling you, as you know the difference, and you recognise controlling behaviour, in all its guises, when you encounter it.

Now you're conscious of how downward focus controls situations you can make choices about how to respond to it. If you recognise its presence, and feel its control is too much, you know it's time to leave the situation, rather than waste any more of your life.

Without the drain of downward focus you've more of yourself available, for yourself and others. You're more open, as the fear of the shadow side no longer controls your actions. This lack of defensiveness means you're able to concentrate far better. You gain clarity when downward focus is no longer stealing your thoughts, distracting your mind, confusing your intentions. So while you have more energy, you're also calmer.

Balance is the perfect state of still water.
Let that be our model.
It remains quiet within
and is not disturbed on the surface

CONFUSCIOUS

Summary

In conclusion, using trust approaches allows you to remove the barrier of downward focus, and to access and develop your inner wisdom and your innate capacity for self-awareness and self-acceptance. The process shines a light onto the shadows in your life and helps you to transform them. You recognise your own shadow, and use its power to benefit your life rather than detract from it; you recognise when others are casting a downward focus shadow over your life, and can protect yourself from it.

The more you free yourself from the constraints of downward focus, the happier you'll be in your own skin, no longer concerned with making sure your mask is in place. This takes a lot of stress out of life. You're less defensive, and consequently more able to share with others. Without the barrier of downward focus drawing your attention and sapping your energy, you can concentrate on where you are now, where you want to go, how you want to get there, and who you want to travel with.

Shadow Man

by Richard Hill

Shadow man, shadow man, how can I know you?
Are you in me, or I in you?
Or are you the candidate's promise of plenty,
Or political truth, or a mirror for two?

Shadow man, shadow man, how can I see you?
Is there a door to go through, can I meet you
Inside the rooms of my mind?

Shadow man, shadow man, dancing in the dark.
Will you help if I ask, if I look in your eyes
Will your gaze overwhelm me and fill me with fear
Of myself - and my dark capacity.

Shadow man, shadow man, come to the light,
Where I can make peace with you, guide to the night
And the grey places within my soul.

Shadow man, shadow man, I will befriend you.
In the union of opposites, paradox works
Like a dream of the ancients.
Listen to their voices!

7 Left Focus

Stop Reason Making Nonsense Of Your Dreams

Explore Left Focus

When left focus becomes a barrier it's because our attention has been drawn by its **dominant influence: logic**.

Left focus is essential in many situations and, of course, using logic to support our decisions is necessary and desirable. But if left focus draws our attention away from a balance with the other focuses—particularly right focus—then it will become a barrier.

Our brains are a big mystery. But it's largely agreed that the left and right hemispheres dance together in a delicate symmetry—very broadly speaking the left is more adept at logical tasks, and the right at creative tasks.

> *If the brain was so simple that we could understand it, we would be so simple that we couldn't*
>
> MICHAEL GRINDER

However, there is no clear divide, and much interplay between the two. To make a distinction, such as whether any individual has a preference for one or other mode of thinking, is over-simplistic. Nevertheless, it's a useful way of conceptualising these different aspects, and BBM borrows from it when defining left focus and right focus.

Left focus is driven by logic—it's literal, analytical, intellectual, objective, rational, and structured. These attributes have been highly prized in our society, and our education system has been geared largely towards left focus, to the exclusion of the more intuitive and abstract right focus. Whether this overemphasis was ever desirable is questionable, but certainly this lack of balance is harmful now.

> *Much of our education,*
> *particularly in the West,*
> *seems to have been designed*
> *to destroy*
> *what is so unique in humanity—*
> *the balance*
> *between our rational*
> *and intuitive selves.*
> *So what have we ended up with?*
>
> **H.R.H. THE PRINCE OF WALES**

We're all acutely aware of rapid change shaking up the world as it was. In virtually all areas of life we're dealing with new ways of doing things, primarily due to the impact of technology. Whereas once we studied to intake information, now we have all the information in the world available at our finger-tips.

Once having information in our heads was vital; now being adept at making connections is a more critical attribute. Not only is learning becoming a new process undertaken with a revised purpose, it's also become something we need to do throughout our lives—which are longer than ever—and not just in our youth. So what we learn, why we learn, how, where, when and for how long we learn has changed. And this changes the skills we need as learners.

> The only truly educated person is the one who has learned how to learn
>
> CARL ROGERS

The skills we need at work are also changing. We can no longer depend on a corporation or institution to nurture us, to provide us with security throughout our working life and a gold watch at the end of it. The expectation of a 'job for life' may already be confined to history. Now redundancy doesn't just unexpectedly visit individual employees; entire industries, even those considered successful and integral to a landscape, are here today, gone tomorrow. Once we might have gone to the same place of work every day, and seen the same colleagues for years; now we're just as likely to work from home, with colleagues in other continents who we connect with daily but never meet in person. We might have grown up believing we'd follow a clear-cut career path, our daily tasks arranged by someone else; now we're increasingly having to design our own career, manage ourselves, be responsible for planning every move we make.

> *No matter where you work,*
> *you are not an employee;*
> *you are in business with one employee—yourself*
> ANDREW S GROVE

Unexpectedly we've gone from predictable stability, to role-hopping, project-hopping, job-hopping, even career-hopping. It's not only today's children who will be doing careers we've not yet heard of; it could be any one of us, tomorrow. We're now in a state of flux, and left focus isn't at all comfortable here. It deals with it by applying logic, while in reality there is only ambiguity.

> *Uproar's your only music*
> KEATS

We have to equip ourselves with the right skills to negotiate an uncertain environment. To undertake the journey successfully demands skills beyond anything asked of most people in the past; skills that our education and training systems recognise but, rooted in left focus thinking, are far from fully embracing.

> *If we learned to walk and talk the way*
> *we are taught how to read and write—*
> *everybody would limp and stutter*
> MARK TWAIN

Employers recognise the need for increased soft skills capabilities in their employees, yet they're nervous of these skills, unsure how to deal with them, develop them, control them, or measure them. Left focus may provide the skills of logic and analysis that are easier to recognise and quantify, but on their own these skills no longer serve us well. Those who realise this, and draw on their other, more mysterious, less quantifiable side, will find themselves in a far better position to ride the waves of change.

It is not the strongest of the species that survive,
not the most intelligent,
but the one most responsive to change

CHARLES DARWIN

Assess Left Focus

When we can recognise left focus, we can assess our life and see if it's holding us back in any way. If left focus is in balance with the other focuses it supports us in making our decisions. Out of balance, left focus constrains us with its insistence on structure and reason, and its denial of anything that can't be seen, proven, or measured to its satisfaction. Left focus makes it impossible for us to follow our dreams, which are intangible by nature. It uses logical reasoning to talk us out of listening to our intuition about what's right for us.

Left focus only responds to functional activities. It needs to have a plan and, crucially, a predictable outcome. It's comfortable with league tables, benchmarks, quotas and the like, and will make them master rather than servant of change. In other words, left focus will use these not to report what has happened, but to direct what will happen. So long as what happens matches its prediction, then left focus will be content; if it doesn't, then left focus will use logic to prove why its prediction should have come true. Many organisations and institutions have this attitude ingrained into their culture, and force compliance to left focus logic, even when it doesn't make sense.

I'll not listen to reason.
Reason always means
what someone else has got to say

ELIZABETH GASKILL

In your work do you have to reach targets?

If so, have you ever reached them by massaging the numbers?

Have you ever been deterred from starting something because you couldn't 'prove' the outcome first?

An outcome that can't be determined before setting out makes left focus very uncomfortable, so experimenting or exploring isn't something it does. It needs to cater for all eventualities before setting off on any venture, neatly packing its proverbial backpack with the most efficient, all-weather gadgets, leaving nothing to chance. Left focus is very comfortable with this sort of controlled activity, so much so that preparation is likely to take longer than the venture itself. And the post-venture reporting needs to be factored in as well. Having put so much effort into planning and post-mortem, left focus becomes irritated if the venture leads to results it hadn't predicted, even positive ones.

We have a plan,
therefore nothing can go wrong
SPIKE MILLIGAN

Do you prefer to know precisely what's going to happen?

In which areas of life is it important to you to be well-prepared?

Do you ever set unrealistic goals, and get annoyed when they're not met?

Do you ever go down a road just to see where it ends up?

Left focus likes a bureaucratic system; it finds pure harmony in a defined framework that to others may seem unwieldy, unclear, even unnecessary. Left focus knows that it's best for a system to control people rather than vice versa, because a system can be built on specific processes with clear functions, and doesn't need to recognise, let alone tolerate the muddle caused by human irrationality. It has stretched this maxim successfully throughout entire countries, making the people slaves to a system.

There's no place for individual thought in the layered, complex bureaucracy of a left focus organisation. Everyone's deterred from it, and has no time for it anyway, busy maintaining the mechanism. Only a very determined individual can find a chink in the bureaucratic armour through which to inject a new idea, only to find it is then whittled out of shape by approval processes and committees.

Employees in a left focus organisation feel powerless to the system. Senior managers are inevitably left focus, assiduously monitoring, assessing and reporting on employees' behaviour. With rewards only given to those who stay in line, employees will either bow down to the system, or bow out, so left focus becomes entrenched at every level.

> The organisations of the future
> will increasingly depend
> on the creativity of their members
> to survive
>
> **WARREN BENNIS**

Have you had to deal with an organisation with this barrier?

If so, how did it make you feel?

Left focus believes that most soft skills are irrelevant, certainly in business. It might be forced to make polite noises about skills like creativity, because they're currently on the political agenda. But creativity makes left focus very 'twitchy': not only is creativity far too unpredictable to contain in any system, but it's something that left focus can't do because it doesn't allow the judgement-free space that's needed to come up with new thinking. If it spots a budding idea, it will set its power of reasoning onto it, and pummel it out of existence.

*If we want to make
the imagination
feel at home,
generosity shows us the way.
How else can imagination thrive
but in a place
where welcoming comes first
and where judgment feels no need to speak
and finally feels
no need to be?*

SARAH WIDER

Are you quick to criticise ideas?

Have you ever used logic to talk yourself out of following a dream?

Left focus lives by the maxim "what gets measured gets done", and believes that the only credible way to measure anything is in a linear, numerical, finite way. Even though its favoured way of measuring can't accurately report the majority of human activity, this is the only method of measuring human activity that makes sense to left focus. As this form of measurement doesn't work with soft skills, left focus has no interest in them.

What things are most important in your life?

How do you measure them?

> All exact science is dominated
> by the idea of approximation
>
> BERTRAND RUSSELL

Here are some thoughts for you to complete spontaneously:

Creative people are...

When I'm playful I feel...

Being adventurous is...

I use my intuition...

If I had more time I'd...

I enjoy my work when I...

Daydreaming is...

If I could do anything I'd...

Meditation is...

A quality I'd like to develop in myself is...

A quality I'd like to let go is...

Something I'd really love to do is...

> Logic will get you from A to B.
> Imagination will take you everywhere else
>
> EINSTEIN

Shift Left Focus

To counteract the impact of left focus use **intuitive approaches**. Look for opportunities to develop your sense of adventure, play, and intuition.

The intuitive approaches you choose to use, and how you apply them, will depend on your own situation.

The following are suggestions for intuitive approaches you can use while reading this book.

Different Day

For one day, see how much you can do differently…just small shifts:

- change what you eat for breakfast

- brush your teeth with your non-dominant hand

- rethink the clothes you put on

- buy a newspaper you never read

- go on a different form of transport from usual

- talk to new people

- go into a type of shop you've not been in before

- change your normal evening activity

- sleep on the other side of the bed.

Playtime

Here are three techniques that can be used together or separately. First time you try it, do them all. Go somewhere you'll be undisturbed for at least 30 minutes.

Come to playtime thinking about a specific situation that you're finding difficult to resolve—maybe a disagreement with someone, a decision you need to reach, a dilemma you want to resolve, or a project that's needs direction.

Play

Put the situation into different circumstances. If you enjoy drawing, put images on paper; otherwise close your eyes, and allow your mind to conjure them. Play with actions, words, ideas and consequences. Let your imagination run riot, seeing the situation being played out in as many of the following contexts as you like:

- a cheesy sitcom
- a speedy cartoon
- an over-the-top opera.

What would the characters look and sound like?

What would they do and say?

How does it make you feel?

Note down any interesting thoughts this provokes.

Adventure

Go back to the original situation.

List eight adventurous ways you could resolve it.

Be as absurd, extraordinary, and outrageous as you like.

Look at the underlying feelings in the list.

Do they tell you anything new?

Is there's anything within the ideas that is feasible.

If so, how could you develop it?

Intuition

Sit comfortably. Contemplate the situation. Close your eyes

Concentrate on your breathing. Follow the breath as it goes in and out.

Relax.

Ask for guidance. Notice the thoughts that come up, but don't judge them.

Let the thoughts move on, bringing your attention back to your breath.

After ten minutes, or whenever you're ready, open your eyes.

Make a note of any thoughts you have.

Playtime over…

Combine observations gained from the three playtime techniques and re-appraise the situation.

Short 'n' Sweet

Do as many of the following activities as possible in one day…

- do one thing to make your work environment more fun

- watch the clouds

- put on lively music in the middle of the day and dance

- go to an art gallery by yourself

- buy a magazine on something you know nothing about

- look in the mirror and pull the silliest face you can

- keep noticing what you've got to be grateful for

- do something you've been putting off

- cook up a new recipe

- whistle

…and do the remaining ones on the following day.

A
spiritual discipline
or meditational practice
which shuns the power of imagination
deprives itself
of the most effective and vital means
of transforming human nature
as it is
into what it could be,
if its dormant potentialities
were fully awakened.

LAMA ANAGARIKA GOVINDA

Creating Goals

Choose one of the goals you wrote down in 'Goals' (page 109). Use creative visualisation to make it more real. This is a very enjoyable form of meditation that draws on your imagination. If you're new to this, you may find that the images you conjur up aren't very clear. Don't struggle, just allow things to come to mind. The more you practise creative visualisation, the clearer the images will become.

Sit comfortably in a quiet place, where you won't be disturbed.

Close your eyes. Relax your body from the toes upwards.

Concentrate on your breathing

Imagine breathing in 'relaxation'; breathing out 'stress' (or any other qualities you choose).

Build a picture in your mind of you achieving your goal.

What does it look like?

Paint the picture as you'd like it to be.

See the colours—turn up the brightness a little.

See yourself in the picture. How do you feel?

What can you hear?

Who else is there?

Add to the scene and enjoy it for as long as you like.

If you have positive affirmations connected to the goal, repeat them to yourself.

When you're ready, put the scene inside a pink bubble.

Let the bubble go...watch it float away.

Ask what your next step should be towards your goal. You may get an answer straight away or sometime later.

When you're ready, gradually open your eyes.

Write down your thoughts and feelings about the goal.

Transform Left Focus

As you use more Intuitive Approaches in your life you'll increasingly access and develop a range of soft skills that get blocked by left focus—the **left focus skills**. These are the skills of creativity, intuition, and imagination.

Most of us have been brought up in a world that impressed upon us the importance of logic over intuition. Analysis, statistics, hard or quantitative evidence are all respected in business, education, and politics. Anything born of logic is considered a superior form of decision-making, even when it contradicts human behaviour; anything born of intuition is seen as a colourful, dispensable poor relation.

> When dealing with people, remember
> you are not dealing with creatures of logic,
> but creatures of emotion
>
> **DALE CARNEGIE**

However, the autonomy of left focus has started to ebb, and forward thinkers believe this movement will continue. Soft skills, once belittled and disregarded, are now seen as the key to living harmoniously in our newly interwoven world.

Using intuitive approaches opens us up to this other side of ourselves, equipping us with essential tools for producing new ideas, forging unexpected connections, exploring innovative solutions, and creating change.

> *Perhaps the macho look*
> *can be interesting*
> *if you want to fight dinosaurs.*
> *But now you need intelligence,*
> *not power and aggression.*
> *Modern intelligence means intuition*
>
> PHILLIPE STARCK

Generating numerous ideas freely is the essential early stage of any creative process; if the left focus voice of reason is allowed in at this point it will destroy all fledgling thoughts. If you hear that left focus voice of reason, whether it's your own or someone else's, show it the door—you can invite it to come back at a later stage. Your first ideas need to flow without fear of judgement. Truly, out of the mouth of babes come new perspectives, so even if you feel ignorant or naïve about something, air your thoughts and see what emerges. And use this openness with others too, so you don't constrain their imagination.

The necessary willingness to look 'foolish' makes this stage one of the hardest to effect in organisations, where left focus invariably predominates, and the pressure is on to perform in a particular way and get quick results.

Every really new idea looks crazy at first
ABRAHAM MASLOW

If you work in left focus situations, practise intuitive approaches on your own to start with, rather than introducing them into a resistant atmosphere. Once you're reaping the rewards brought by having such 'foolishness' as second nature, you'll be better positioned to take it into your work environment.

Listening To Your Intuition

A hunch
is creativity
trying to tell you something
FRANK CAPRA

Turning down the volume on the stern voice of left focus allows you to hear your intuition. There are various techniques that can make it even clearer to you.

Meditation

This is a guaranteed route to your inner voice—just 10 minutes a day can change your life.

> This sows the seeds
> that enable us to be more awake
> in the midst of everyday chaos
>
> PEMA CHODRON

Dreams

These are a wonderful source of raw data. We spend so much time sleeping and processing our waking hours, that there's a treasure trove of insight here. You don't need a complicated interpretation to learn from it—you're your own expert. The emotions in your dreams hold the best clues. Keep a notebook next to your bed and see if you can develop the habit of noting down your dreams immediately when you wake up.

Gut responses

These are the most direct interpreters of your emotions. In 'Under Words' (page 104) you tuned into how your body felt when you were talking to people. You can use this same technique with anything in your life. Hear what your gut tells you. It's part of your decision-making process that's at least as intelligent as your rational response.

> Innovation
> is both conceptual
> and perceptual...
> successful innovators
> use both the right side
> and the left side
> of their brains.
> They look at figures
> and they look at people.
>
> PETER DRUCKER

Let your ideas 'free fall'

Make time to use your imagination actively but without any particular function in mind. Left focus will get irate at this; it will nag you to think of a reason, tell you that you're wasting time. But the longer you can hold out and just play with an idea, the more you exercise this part of your mind.

Daydream

Listen to shadow patterns, watch the pictures your thoughts say. A few minutes a day here is time well spent.

Boost your creative thinking

Do some research into techniques that can help this; experiment with them. Avoid labelling yourself as having a preference—preferences change as circumstances change, and often things we're uncomfortable with produce the more interesting result.

136

> To live a creative life,
> we must lose our fear of being wrong
>
> JOSEPH CHILTON PEARCE

Delve into 'what if' ideas

Consider ideas like 'what if no one ate meat?' Or 'what if I women had more muscle power than men?' Or 'what if I got rid of my car and got a donkey instead?'

Get into the habit of 'mulling'

Put the specifics of a problem you have into a question. Then go and do something completely different. See how quickly the solution pops into your head.

Change your habits in small ways, **nudging yourself out of 'thinking ruts':**

- Invite someone to coffee, just because they're very different to you.
- Try on a pair of outrageously expensive shoes.
- Collaborate with someone new on a small project.
- Wander round an antique shop.
- Stop and listen to a busker.
- Make up the life stories of strangers you're travelling with.
- Take a small bit of nature home…a leaf, stone, flower.

Do not fear mistakes.
There are none

MILES DAVIS

Record And Edit Your Ideas

When you generate ideas, you need to be prepared to record them. Have plenty of ways to hand, so you can always find the method that suits you and the idea—write them down, make graphic representations, use software, record or film them. Make sure the method doesn't direct the idea—left focus is always trying to find ways to be in control, so tame its impulse.

Once your ideas are recorded in an unrestricted way, give yourself time to mull them. The brain does a lot of work on its own so, if you can, give it space to sift through what you've come up with. Again, check logic isn't interfering and stopping you from allowing enough time for this.

Our brains are very active when we
daydream—much more active
than when we focus on routine tasks

KALINA CHRISTOFF

When it's time to edit, allow your intuition to be ruthless. You've made a record of your ideas so nothing's lost, and you'll have sketches of discarded ideas to use another time.

Only then bring left focus thinking into the process—to help shape the specifics, do the planning, build the system, and execute the idea.

In the long run men only hit what they aim at
HENRY DAVID THOREAU

Goal Setting

Goal setting has become one of the most familiar themes in personal development and business management literature. There are few that counter, for example, the SMART acronym, which reminds us that goals should be specific, measurable, attainable, realistic, and time-bound. If you wish to take this approach there's a great deal of information to help you. You can still use BBM effectively in conjunction with it, particularly as a primer. However, BBM comes at goal setting from a slightly different perspective.

By working through the BBM process, you won't need to set goals in a rigid way, nor strive to achieve them. You'll have to make plans and take action of course, but you do this with ease when you recognise and remove barriers that could hold you back, when you're in alignment with your goals, and when you truly wish to achieve them. You then see a goal as a landscape you're excited about visiting and are intrinsically motivated to move towards. This creates enthusiasm, an eagerness to take on the challenge and establish the milestones to get there, plus the energy to take the necessary steps towards it.

Goal setting dominated by left focus has some inherent flaws. For instance, if you treat a goal as sacrosanct, you limit yourself by discounting alternatives without due consideration. And if left focus blinkers you to everything but the goal, you miss the journey. Yet the journey may be all you have, as even the best planned goals aren't always reached.

> *Life is what's happening*
> *while we're busy making other plans*
> **JOHN LENNON**

Not achieving a particular long-term goal will cause depression if left focus is in the driving seat—a primary cause of depression is a mismatch between reality as it is, and reality as we think it should be. And even if you do make it to your goal, you may find it falls short of your expectations.

> *Achievement brings its own anticlimax.*
> **MAYA ANGELOU**

140

It's not only personal goal setting that can be negatively affected by left focus; there is growing concern that the current approach to goal setting in organisations is damaging, with a recent Harvard Business School Report[1] concluding that it can "degrade employee performance, shift focus away from important but non-specified goals, harm interpersonal relationships, corrode organizational culture, and motivate risky and unethical behaviours".

Even though the BBM approach increases the likelihood that you'll reach your destination, it makes enjoying the journey the priority. It encourages you to recognise that your journey is likely to lead you in unexpected directions, to be prepared for this, and to travel with the awareness that if you do reach your goal it may not be as you imagined.

*A passionate mind
is seeking,
overcoming,
not accepting any tradition;
it is not
a decided mind,
not a mind
that has arrived,
but it is a young mind
that is ever arriving*

JIDDU KRISHNAMURTI

---

1 Ordóñez, L. et al. (2009) "Goals Gone Wild: The Systematic Side Effects of Over-Prescribing Goal Setting". Working Paper 09-083. Harvard Business School.

Summary

In conclusion, if you let left focus take control too early it will be a barrier, making you set goals you think you should achieve, but that you don't care about with passion; goals that are a logical next step, but that don't make your heart sing; goals that are safe or practical, but that aren't in line with your purpose.

Intuitive approaches allow you to remove the barrier of left focus, and tap into your creativity and intuition, quietening the critical voice of reason, and freeing your flow of ideas.

You develop ideas by listening to your intuitive responses, your dreams, and your gut reactions, drawing on your life experience, and sculpting your individual perspective. You can make even more of your store of ideas by using techniques to ensure you don't get into thinking 'ruts', jolting your imagination to keep it active. Generating numerous ideas, even if they're totally 'off the wall', gives your mind plenty of material to play with, to mull and mould. By now you will have many ways of recording these ideas, so you can keep stocking up your creative storehouse, to dip into whenever you choose.

The goals that emerge from this kind of thinking are packed with rich reasons for you to achieve them. This desire automatically fires up the motivation you need to plan the journey, and the enthusiasm and energy to get you on the road.

Each Life Converges to some Centre

by Emily Dickinson

Each life converges to some centre
Expressed or still;
Exists in every human nature
A goal,

Admitted scarcely to itself, it may be,
Too fair
For credibility's temerity
To dare.

Adored with caution, as a brittle heaven,
To reach
Were hopeless as the rainbow's raiment
To touch,

Yet persevered toward, surer for the distance;
How high
Unto the saints' slow diligence
The sky!

Ungained, it may be, by a life's low venture,
But then,
Eternity enables the endeavouring
Again.

8 Right Focus

Moving Ideas From Fantasy To Fact

Explore Right Focus

When right focus becomes a barrier it's because our attention has been drawn by its

dominant influence: imagination

> *Creation is only the projection into form of that which already exists*
>
> SHRIMAD BHAGAVATAM

Imagination is our inexhaustible source of wisdom and our freedom, taking us beyond ourselves. But, as with all the dominant influences, if it draws our attention out of balance with the other focuses—particularly left focus—then it will become a barrier.

Right focus inhabits a non-linear plane; it's abstract, intuitive, metaphorical, creative, subjective, emotional, and flexible. Because these qualities are increasingly important, and historically have been underused and undervalued, right focus can handle more attention than the other focuses before becoming a barrier.

However, right focus still needs to be in balance, otherwise its ephemeral nature will take over and its full value will evaporate.

We're all creative; it is an inherent human capability. As small children creativity was our energy, tickling us to try things, to experiment and explore, to talk and walk and play.

> *The secret of genius*
> *is to carry the spirit of childhood*
> *into maturity*
>
> **VERNON LAW**

Throughout childhood that sense of curiosity and adventure is gradually buried under the weight of others' expectations, our self-consciousness, and left focus reasoning. But, as with all soft skills blocked by barriers, our creativity is still there, waiting to be accessed.

As its key role in our new world has become increasingly apparent, creativity has been given greater attention. It's now revered in places where it was once reviled, lauded by politicians, academics and the business world. However, despite this recently elevated status, creativity is still subject to misunderstanding and mistrust, largely because it was sidelined from the mainstream for so long, and associated almost exclusively with a bohemian way of life.

Society has long looked upon artists with suspicion, understanding neither their lifestyle, nor their skills. But their lifestyle and skills now have something to teach us all. In a society no longer buffered by secure incomes and clear-cut career paths, we need a completely new skill set. These skills, such as self-motivation, flexibility, initiative, teamwork, and creativity, are those which have always been central to the artist's lifestyle—one that is no longer just for mavaricks, but is streaming into the core of normality.

Artists trade in creativity, a skill that has been thought of as random, spontaneous, uncontrollable; hence artists have been similarly labelled. But every artist knows that they must structure their creativity for it to flourish. At each step of the creative process the artist must construct a framework to carry the results of their creative endeavour, or it will dissolve to nothing.

> *Do we not find freedom along the guiding lines of discipline?*
> YEHUDI MENUHIN

At the very start of the creative process, an artist chooses their medium, and the structure within which the creativity moves from mind into matter: the painter chooses a particular canvas, the composer a musical form, the writer a format... each confines their creativity before they begin. This balance between creativity and structure is as essential to the process as balance between consonance and disso-nance, conflict and resolution, light and shade are essential to the work itself.

Let's go right to the end of the process—where the finished work is presented: the painter's exhibition doesn't happen without persistence and planning; to rehearse, record, and perform the composition requires discipline, dedication, and determination; to get the play on stage needs efficient project and time management. All these are structures within which the creativity is contained and communicated.

As change propels us forward into a new age there's much we can learn from the artists' way of working, not least of which is how to use structure to support our abstract thinking. If we don't give right focus clear boundaries, it distracts and disrupts us, no longer a benefit but a barrier.

> *A work of art*
> *is not a matter*
> *of thinking beautiful thoughts*
> *or experiencing tender emotions*
> *(though those are its raw materials),*
> *but of intelligence,*
> *skill,*
> *taste,*
> *proportion,*
> *knowledge,*
> *discipline*
> *and industry;*
> *especially discipline.*
>
> **EVELYN WAUGH**

Assess Right Focus

When we recognise right focus, we can assess our life and see if it's holding us back in any way. We know if right focus is in balance with the other focuses, particularly left focus, when we've systems and structures that give life clarity of purpose, help us make the most of our time, and frame our energies effectively. If right focus is out of balance, then disorder and lack of direction squander our talents and hold us back from achieving our potential.

Right focus has numerous ideas, makes interesting connections, and thinks up unusual solutions, but it's unable to move concepts into form, so nothing it conceptualises gets realised. Many people find the barrier presents itself as poor time management. Right focus resents having to keep to a schedule, although this rarely means it errs on the side of being early; it's notoriously late. Its persistent unpunctuality comes across as inconsiderate and disrespectful of others' time, although right focus really doesn't intend this.

How's your time management?

Are you generally on time, or known for being late?

Are you late for some but not for others? If so, how do you discriminate?

Are you rushed a lot of the time? If yes, why?

Right focus eats time. The time is there, but everything is so ill-paced that life turns into a chaotic frenzy, careering headlong from one deadline to another.

149

Do you believe that you perform better under pressure?

Some may try to reason with right focus about its timekeeping, using logic to point out the negative impact that the behaviour has. But right focus doesn't do logic, so this approach has no effect. Whether or not there's any conscious intent to control, this is the effect the behaviour has…others are forced to plan around right focus at every step.

Do others in your life have to pick up your slack?
Are you expected to pick up someone else's slack?

If anything needs planning, you can't expect right focus to be a part of it. It's not that right focus is incapable or lazy; it simply prefers either to avoid the task, or to find someone else to do it.

Even the simplest family get-together involves too many practical considerations to be bothered with, so something as complicated as financial planning is way off the scale for right focus, leading to the inevitable consequences.

> My bonds and shares
> May fall downstairs
> Who cares, who cares
> I'm dancing and I can't be bothered now
>
> IRA GERSHWIN

Do you dislike planning, enjoy it, or do it just because you have to?

Are you self-motivated?

In business, a lack of planning and processes, financial and otherwise, has disastrous repercussions. To the outside observer, an organisation with right focus may look like a cool place to work because it's not bogged down by red tape or protocol, it generates ideas, and it's open to concepts such as diversity and creativity. But the right focus organisation lacks the mechanisms through which to put any of this into effective practice.

> It will not do
> to leave a live dragon out of your plans
> if you live near one.
>
> J R TOLKEIN

In fact, the lack of processes can work against the very concepts such organisations would appear to support; for example, without procedures to ensure accountability, discriminatory behaviour can happen without question or consequence.

Working for an organisation affected by right focus is like being in a boat on a river without any banks. The lack of clarity stretches from the ethos, right through all the systems, to the outcomes.

151

Have you worked for an organisation of this kind?

If so, what effect did it have on you?

It's impossible for right focus to concentrate on one objective, let alone to formulate an overarching strategy. Whatever it achieves is haphazard, its route a tangle of spaghetti junctions. For employees, this is frustrating and de-motivating, an uncertain hit-and-miss process of second guessing. Professionally and personally, outcomes are random when you've only the vaguest idea of where you're going, and not the foggiest idea of how you'll get there.

> Enthusiasm
> can only be aroused
> by two things:
> first,
> an ideal,
> which takes the imagination by storm,
> and second,
> a definite intelligible plan
> for carrying that ideal into practice.
>
> **ARNOLD TOYNBEE**

Right focus gets waylaid by all sorts of distractions—from issues connected to a task but of little importance, to entirely unrelated whims and fancies. Its attention is a flibbertigibbet, so nothing is completed unless by fluke.

If you get sidetracked, is it usually beneficial, or a waste of time?

Is your work space organised so you can always find what you need?

Right focus finds nothing remotely appealing about setting up systems, and even less in maintaining them. At home and at work, disorder is everywhere, and there's no system hidden within the mess.

Right focus loses things all the time, and can't use logic to deduce that hunting for stuff is the most enervating of activities. It disparages as mundane and petty the pleading from those who have to share its space—or, as is more often the case, its lack of space.

Are you often frustrated by misplacing things?

Does your life feel cluttered?

Does anyone else's mess get in your way?

Right focus wastes potential by distracting attention and dissipating energy. Individuals may achieve by chance, but an organisation affected by right focus cannot grow beyond a certain point before a lack of strategic aims and clear leadership causes ideas and talent, then the organisation itself, to disappear.

The object of all work
is production
or accomplishment
and to either of these ends
there must be forethought,
system,
planning,
intelligence,
and honest purpose,
as well as perspiration.

THOMAS EDISON

Here are some thoughts for you to complete spontaneously:

Working on my own is...

Deadlines are...

Making my own decisions is...

My biggest timewaster is...

When I promote myself to others I feel...

If I had more time I'd like to...

My time keeping at work is...

My time keeping with friends and family is...

When other people tell me what to do I feel...

When I tell other people what to do I feel...

My life is as organised as...

My financial planning is...

I am most self motivated when...

My goal setting is...

When I finish a project I'm...

My daily schedule is...

Shift Right Focus

To counteract the impact of right focus use **structured approaches**. These allow us to clarify our thinking, remove clutter, set up frameworks, define aims, and design strategies. Those you choose to use, and how you apply them, will depend on your own situation.

Suggestions for some structured approaches you can use while reading this book are set out below.

Do The Research

Poor time management is a common cause of stress, and this isn't surprising. We live in a world where we're increasingly required to sculpt our own lives, yet we're unlikely to have ever been shown how to manage our time effectively. Many school leavers are shocked by the level of self-organisation that's demanded of them at college or in work; similarly someone who's been made redundant, and chosen to become self-employed, can find managing themselves for the first time surprisingly difficult.

Many of us feel our skills aren't sufficient for today's needs, and our sense of inadequacy leads to overwhelm and self-recrimination, as if poor time management is an inherent personality trait. But if we've spent our lifetime being told by others what to do, when to do it, and pestered if we don't, then working on our own initiative and designing our own schedule is simply something we've not been educated to do and are ill-prepared for. So, teach yourself.

In a matter of hours you can learn techniques that will save you years in the long run. However, to get the best outcome it is crucial that you find systems that work for you (see 'Systems Analysis' below) rather than struggling to make yourself fit a particular system.

Whatever your level of ability there are always more tips to pick up, so make this an ongoing habit; accept this as an integral part of your lifelong learning plan.

Time is our most precious resource; spending it wisely is the key to being efficient, relaxed, and happy.

> *You can't earn more time*
> *regardless of how hard you work*
>
> **ERNIE ZELINSKI**

Systems Analysis

Whichever time management and organisational techniques you come across, you need to make them work for you. Never assume that any system should work well for you in practice, however promising it seems, or however much it's 'sold' to you. If one fails, it doesn't mean you're doomed to be forever disorganised, it just means that the system didn't suit you. Try another.

Sometimes circumstances force us to adapt to a pre-existing system—but if you can, adapt the system to suit you. Look for systems that suit your needs and, above all else, your temperament. This process takes trial, error, and imagination.

Three simple steps to help you analyse the way you organise, to find out how you can make your personal systems more effective and enjoyable are set out below.

What works well?

Even the most disorganised of us have some aspect of our lives, however small, that we happily keep on track. Identify one of your existing systems that works well.

What is it that encourages you to do this particular system?

What do you enjoy about it?

Which part of your personality does it tap into?

Consider how you can adapt this approach to address an aspect of your life that isn't working so smoothly.

In ev'ry job that must be done
There is an element of fun
You find the fun and snap!
The job's a game

MARY POPPINS

Where do you get pile-ups?

Identify one place where you always get a backlog of 'stuff' piling up, and where tidying becomes a chore.

What sort of stuff is it?

Why exactly does this blockage happen?

To get any system flowing you want each step to nudge you on to the next one, so you hardly have to think about. You don't want to tidy it, and then have it happen again; you want to create a system that makes everything flow easily, so it will never be necessary to 'tidy' it again.

What can you put into place that will unblock this?

Once you've set up the system, test it. See how it settles in.

Does it work?

If it doesn't, tweak it or try something new.

If it does, where else can you apply the same principle?

What do you lose?

Identify just one item that you mislay regularly.

Give it a home and make sure it's always put there.

Take your time to get it settled in

Choose something else. Keep going.

Mind Games

Exercising the brain is as important as exercising the body. There's no physical reason why our intellects cannot keep growing, and our cognitive abilities continue to improve. But if we don't use our brain, we lose it; if we don't keep it in shape it will atrophy.

> One way to compensate
> for a tiny brain
> is to pretend to be dead.
>
> SCOTT ADAMS

Learning is the best means of keeping a brain fit, but doing familiar activities in new ways is also very beneficial. Try the following mind games.

Questions

First, spend a day being really aware of how you ask questions.

Then, spend a day asking as many questions as you reasonably can—ask yourself and others.

Ask open questions—those that cannot be answered with 'yes' or 'no'.

Use: Who? What? Why? When? Where? Which? How?

Do you make use of all of these?

Keep going deeper into any problem by asking questions.

At the end of the day, ask yourself about the effects this had.

Write down your thoughts.

Dictionary

Every day for a week, open the dictionary; pick any new word you fancy.

Write it down.

Learn it.

Use it.

Put a dictionary in the bathroom., with a book of brain teasers, and a joke book.

> *Making the simple complicated is commonplace;*
> *making the complicated simple,*
> *awesomely simple,*
> *that's creativity*
>
> **CHARLES MINGUS**

Top Time Tips

- Keep things simple.

- Set priorities–dont let the 'small stuff' drain your time.

- Schedule each day, with room for flexibility.

- Make sure you build in time to play.

- Choose your activities wisely–go for quality not quantity.

- Avoid distractions.

- Watch less TV.

- If an email can be dealt with in less than two minutes, do it.

- Master time by being present in the moment. Practise mindfulness.

- Slow down.

Transform Right Focus

As you use more structured approaches in your life you'll shift towards forward focus. With this, you increasingly access and develop a range of soft skills that get blocked by right focus—the **right focus skills**. These are skills that help you build structures to make the best use of your time, space, actions, thoughts and imagination.

> *An idea that is developed*
> *and put into action*
> *is more important*
> *than an idea that exists only as an idea.*
>
> BUDDHA

At first glance you might think right focus quite a benign barrier, given that its dominant influence is imagination. But consider how much damage it can cause: poor time management, a messy environment, chaotic activities, muddled thoughts and wasted ideas are some of the effects of right focus in action.

Right focus has various justifications for its stance; a favourite is that too much organising would rein in its free spirit, inhibit its individuality, its creativity. Although this argument suggests a positive intention, it's actually based on an aversion to anything left focus, and presupposes that getting organised is an uncreative activity for dull people. But the way you organise yourself is just as individual as you are; it's whatever you make it.

> *Shakespeare*
> *wrote his sonnets*
> *within a strict discipline,*
> *fourteen lines of iambic pentameter,*
> *rhyming in three quatrains and a couplet.*
> *Were his sonnets dull?*
>
> *Mozart wrote his sonatas*
> *within an equally rigid discipline—*
> *exposition, development, and recapitulation.*
> *Were they dull?*
>
> **DAVID OGILVY**

Repetitive or mundane tasks give us the opportunity to use our brains in ways precluded by more involving work. If you've an idea to mull over, a decision to reach, or a problem to solve, this is the time to undertake a repetitive task. Don't look on this as procrastination, because it isn't. Do it guilt-free. Keep the issue in mind, but take a break from actively thinking about it and allow your brain to change gear. While you're doing something else—filing, tidying up, data entry, practising scales—your brain will still be processing, and will often deliver the solution to you spontaneously, or the moment you put your attention back to the issue.

Have a stock of essential, routine activities that you can build into the more demanding tasks as 'brain-breaks', a type of moving meditation. By combining different tasks you create structures that are more productive and more enjoyable.

Virtually every activity requires preparation beforehand and clear-up afterwards, which are unlikely to be as interesting as the activity itself. This is a favourite right focus excuse for putting-off seemingly appealing activities. However, if we accept that preparation and clear-up are integral to tasks, we can pre-plan how to make them enjoyable, so rather than deterring us from a task, they act as an incentive. Ask yourself what you can do to make more of this time. Depending on what it involves, could you listen to music? Or make easy phone calls? Could you listen to a radio programme that interests you, or hear a podcast you've recorded? Think about options that act as an incentive.

Motivate yourself—and others—with the promise of a small treat once a task has been completed. Our brain is very responsive to our own 'bribes'. These can be extremely simple as our brains don't need big rewards to feel satisfied. A cup of coffee, listening to music, a chat—many kinds of small treats will tease it along.

> *Joyful listening to music activates the reward system of the brain and leads to release of dopamine.*
> NATIONAL ACADEMY OF SCIENCES

Completing a task, without a mess left in its wake, brings with it a sense of satisfaction that in itself is habit forming. If you find yourself picking up after someone who's quite capable of doing it for themselves, then you've fallen prey to a right focus ploy. Ask yourself why you're doing it. You're not only wasting your own time, but you're also denying another the opportunity to develop habits that, in the longer term, make the everyday parts of their life more meaningful. For example, if an adult integrates routine tasks with something enjoyable, and presents them in a positive way, then a child will do them quite happily; in the process the child becomes used to doing the tasks, becomes more adept at them, and learns a valuable approach to time management and organising. Alternatively, present something as a 'chore' and that's what it will always be.

> Work is either fun or drudgery.
> It depends on your attitude.
> I like fun.
>
> COLLEEN C. BARRETT

When you see something as a chore you'll need self-discipline, in its strictest, finger-wagging sense, to get yourself to do it. But if you've habituated yourself to think more creatively about how you do tasks, and have become more motivated by making a clear link between the routine task and your 'bigger picture', then self-discipline takes on a gentler face. You'll do tasks willingly if you've designed systems and structures that really work for you. To others you appear incredibly self-disciplined; all the while you're getting a buzz, enjoying the process of getting where you want to go.

> Find a job you love
> and you add five days to every week
>
> H. JACKSON BROWN JNR

In any goal-setting process, and particularly with personal goals, trust your inner voice; hear what makes your heart sing, and recognise what gives you a sense of purpose. Make this your starting point. With these in alignment, goals come naturally—you'll know what you want to do and why you want to do it. And you'll be motivated from within yourself to achieve it. This inner drive is the vital force you need to get through any disappointments, rejection, delays and doubts you'll encounter along the way. Once your goals have become clear, design the systems and structures you need for the journey. Make sure these are the servant, not the master, of your goals.

Structured approaches aren't only useful for organising the nuts and bolts of your activities; they're also valuable for framing your imagination, recording your ideas, turning thoughts into substance and fleshing out your ambitions. Use structured approaches to record ideas, making sure that you don't choose a system that forces you to tamper with the idea just to suit the system's requirements. Keep looking for new techniques you can use—with a range of them at your fingertips you're more likely to stay true to an idea, rather than having to bend it out of shape simply to fit a particular system. For example, Mind Maps provide a way of recording thoughts that's attuned to the way we think—free-flowing and individualistic. It's a useful technique that you can apply in numerous situations—from ad-hoc meetings, to detailed project planning at home or work. Technology offers a slew of useful tools, and the key is to find ones that suit you, that are easy to use and, crucially, that you continue to use over time. This only comes about through first researching to find what suits your needs, and then experimenting to discover which suits your personality.

Whatever tools you use, make the process as streamlined as possible, so the filing and retrieval of ideas is easy and intuitive. After trialling something, if you find it's not 'stuck', assess why it's not working for you, and adapt it; or just let it go and try something else…you'll know when you find the right system for you, because you'll enjoy using it, so you'll keep using it.

If this research process is frustrating, that's a good sign—it means you're really aligned with your goals and eager to move. Be patient. You don't want to bend yourself out of shape any more than you want to bend your ideas out of shape. However, if you suspect you might be using the process to procrastinate, this is an indication that your goals need looking at again, to identify which barriers are holding you back.

> *I am not discouraged,*
> *because every wrong attempt discarded*
> *is another step forward*
>
> **THOMAS EDISON**

Have plenty of notebooks and pens around your space, always within easy reach—a lo-tech, highly effective aid. Keeping new ideas 'analog' rather than 'digital' gives them more room to breathe in the early stages. And you want to be able to jot down any thoughts or ideas you have as soon as possible and in a rough form, whether you get it in an interesting dream, in the shower, or in the middle of a film. Get it on paper and, unless it requires urgent attention, tear out the page, put it in your in-tray along with the non-urgent 'stuff' that you deal with once a week; then allow the brain to mull it. When you revisit the idea, transfer it to the appropriate system if it still looks interesting; if you thnk it's of no value, bin it.

No amount of skilful invention can replace the essential element of imagination

EDWARD HOPPER

Once your imagination has been allowed the judgement-free space, or mulling time, within which to develop an idea, it's ready for the editing phase, when structured approaches can be introduced. However, they really come into their own in the planning phase. This is the time to:

- Discuss and analyse the choices you're making.
- Ask yourself or others plenty of open-ended questions to get deep into the issues.
- Write summaries to cut through to the elemental points.
- Make action plans with milestones to help keep you on track.
- Set up whichever task or project management method you use.

And then set off.

> Life isn't a matter of milestones
> but of moments
>
> ROSE KENNEDY

Summary

In conclusion, structured approaches allow you to remove the barrier of right focus, and design the best systems to support your life, not rule it. This process allows you to identify where your time, ideas, and energies are being dissipated because you're not holding them in the best 'containers'.

Rather than seeing it as a boring duty, you choose to incorporate organisation as part of the creative process, seeing it as an opportunity to make the most of your ideas, and to turn mundane chores into useful brain breaks.

You design systems that suit your needs and your personality, so they're enjoyable and they motivate you, rather than control or stifle you. And you no longer get frustrated, wasting your time hunting amongst clutter.

Rethinking how you structure tasks includes having a stockpile of routine jobs to intersperse with the more interesting and involving tasks, taking guilt-free breaks, and knowing how to reward yourself when a job's completed.

You balance right and left focus, allowing ideas to flow freely into the best containers to hold them. With plenty of options and techniques at the ready, you never bend yourself or your ideas out of shape to suit a system. You get more done, more efficiently, more effectively, more enjoyably.

Cool Rule

by Peter Firebrace

Some say rules and regulations provide the foundations

Others say "Me, I need to be free from all that!

Discipline is boring, I just start snoring

And all I want's to get away and take a nap!"

So let it all go and go with the flow?

Or work it and work it and get it just so?

Be precise! Be exact! Don't be happy with fuzzy!

Who wants to listen to something that's mushy and muzzy?

Be tight, not uptight! Be right on the beat!

Let the rhythm flow through you, tap it out with your feet!

Let the melody flow and get it just so!

Who said that you had to choose?

Be strict, even rigid - it doesn't mean you're frigid

Just that the structure is strong and not loose!

9 Moving On...

Introduction

BBM is an approach to life that you can adapt and adopt as suits you. The more you use it, the more you'll want to use it. Why? Simply, because it makes life so much more enjoyable!

BBM doesn't pretend that life will be without problems. On the contrary, it accepts that problems are an inevitable part of life, and it prepares you for the only thing that you can expect in life—the unexpected.

You don't know what is going to happen tomorrow.
Life is a crazy ride,
and nothing is guaranteed

EMINEM

Through its five lenses—the **barrier profiles**—you not only see problems more clearly, but also find the solutions inside yourself. BBM gives you mastery over the barriers you'll encounter on your journey. You're ready for whatever happens tomorrow, so you're free to enjoy today and to live fully in the moment.

You can use the mechanism of the five barrier profiles in various ways. By reading this book and doing the exercises you've no doubt spotted particular barriers you'd like to concentrate on.

Which barrier or barriers 'spoke' to you most strongly?

What actions are you going to take next?

Make a note of your 'next moves'. If you've been keeping a journal, now is a good time to look through it to remind yourself of everything you've done, and to remember the various thoughts and ideas you've had along the way.

As well as using the barrier profiles generally in your life, you can also use them as lenses through which to view a specific issue; whether you're dealing with change at home or challenges at work; differences with friends, family, or colleagues; personal issues concerning your direction, motivation or confidence. The BBM process used in this book—Explore, Assess, Shift, Transform—ensures you view an issue from all perspectives. Here's a reminder of each stage:

Explore

At this stage you consider each focus profile, reminding yourself of their dominant influences and characteristics, and directing them generally towards your current issue. See Table 9.1.

Table 9.1 Focus Profiles: dominant influence

Focus	Dominant Influence
Backward	*Past*
Inward	*Self*
Downward	*Shadow*
Left	*Logic*
Right	*Imagination*

If you'd like to deepen your understanding of the five focus profiles, you can supplement material in this book with resources from www.barrierbreakers.co.uk.

Assess

During the assess stage you scrutinise your current issue through the lens of each focus, to see if the focus is working harmoniously, or whether it's causing a barrier.

The questions in this book and in the accompanying journal can be revisited and related to your particular issue. Make a note of the revised questions as well as your answers. Depending on the depth of the issue, you could just do a quick scan with each focus; or you may want to continue using the journal, as a useful way to clarify your assessment, and to gauge how your perception changes over time. If you need to make a more expansive assessment of the issue, you can use techniques you developed throughout the book to organise and record your observations.

Assess all five focuses, rather than make any assumptions beforehand about which are the more relevant. Barriers are often obfuscated and need prodding before they reveal themselves. Upon completing the assess stage you'll have identified which focuses have become barriers—usually one or two. If you find more than this, it's best to 'chunk' the issue into smaller parts, so you can concentrate on each barrier in turn.

Shift

Now you've identified which focus has become a barrier, your goal is to swing attention away from its dominating influence, and back into the balance of forward focus. You achieve this by applying the relevant counteracting approach.

The counteracting approaches in this book will have given you many ideas. Use these as a guide to develop your own counteracting approaches—you get the best results when you design opportunities that relate directly to you and your specific issue.

Some reminders of the key features of each counteracting approach are shown in Table 9.2.

Table 9.2 Key features of counteracting approaches

Focus	Counteracting approach	Where there are opportunities to:
Backward	*Self-referring*	*Recognise and develop your own opinions, thoughts, feelings, and identity, and to detach these from the dominating influence of others and the past*
Inward	*Empathic*	*Turn your attention towards others, to understand their circumstances, consider things from their perspective and respond productively to them*
Downward	*Trust*	*Recognise and deepen your connection to your inner wisdom, to identify and free yourself from limiting emotions and behaviours*
Left	*Intuitive*	*Develop your sense of adventure, play, and intuition, to put your imagination to work, and to inject creativity into all aspects of your life*
Right	*Structured*	*Design and establish systems and structures that suit your needs and personality, to clarify your thinking, contain your creativity, remove clutter, support your purpose, and organize your actions*

As well as creating opportunities for yourself, you may wish to do the same for others. If so, don't expect or demand anyone else's growth. Instead, aim to set up environments designed around particular counteracting approaches, where a seed of change can find nourishment and be allowed to grow in its own time and direction.

175

Transform

Once you've applied your counteracting approaches you'll want to keep checking to see if they're working effectively and to determine whether any adjustments could be made. Remember, BBM encourages you to take a flexible, on-going approach, so you adapt in response to circumstances—changing something does not imply it was incorrect beforehand. The transform stage allows you to review your environment over time, to see if the opportunities you've created are having the intended effect, and to ensure that the relevant soft skills are being accessed and developed.

Here's a reminder of the transformation brought about by overcoming each barrier.

Backward Focus Skills

These realign you to who you truly are—your beliefs, your purpose, and what you want from life. They strengthen your ability to lead yourself and others, and are the key skills for making and managing change. The skills you'll access and develop include independent judgement, questioning, self-reliance, and leadership.

It's never too late
to be what you might have been

GEORGE ELIOT

Inward Focus Skills

These connect you to others and to life beyond yourself. They improve your communication at every level, enabling you to understand others, to develop and deepen positive relationships, and to recognise and disengage from those that attempt to control you. The skills you'll access and develop include teamwork, listening, social interaction, and negotiating.

If a man
be gracious
to strangers,
it shows that he is
a citizen of the world,
and his heart is no island,
cut off from other islands,
but a continent that joins them

FRANCIS BACON

Downward Focus Skills

These allow your actions to be guided by your inner wisdom, rather than by under-lying fears. This brings peace of mind, improved energy, and clarity of direction. You trust yourself, knowing how to use the best of your shadow side, and how to shine a light on any other shadows cast over your life. The skills you'll access and develop include assertiveness, concentration, motivation, and confidence.

> *Some of the pure gold*
> *of our personality*
> *is relegated to the shadow*
> *because it can find no place*
> *in that great levelling process*
> *that is culture*
>
> **ROBERT A JOHNSON**

Left Focus Skills

These access and work with your intuition and creativity, encouraging aware-ness and enjoyment of the present moment, building a vision that's born of your passion and purpose, and allowing you to travel comfortably with uncertainty, responding to life's challenges with flexibility and imagination. The skills you'll access and develop include idea generation, creative thinking, problem solving, and intuitive responses.

*I can't understand
why people are frightened
of new ideas.
I'm frightened of the old ones*

JOHN CAGE

Right Focus Skills

These allow you to set up the best systems to get you where you wish to go. They help you design ways to hold your ideas, your time, and your actions, so you make the most of these precious resources, while feeling relaxed and supported. The skills you'll access and develop include self-discipline, critical reasoning, decision making, and time management.

*Beautiful systems foster
rather than quash
innovation*

TOM PETERS

Summary

Getting into a habit of using the five focuses as 'lenses' makes it ever easier to navigate barriers, allowing you to recognise and remove those already in your life, and dealing with new ones before they inhibit your progress.

Sometimes a situation will need greater scrutiny, and this is when you can use EAST. Each stage of the EAST process has a different function, providing you with a simple route through which to identify and overcome the barriers in even the most complex situation.

At the explore stage you remind yourself of the composition of each focus and what causes it to become a barrier, giving you time to reflect on how these might relate to your current situation. During the assess stage you drill down deeper into the situation, examining it through the lens of each focus, to identify which has become a barrier, and what inhibitors have been produced. You're then ready to enter the shift stage, when you design and apply counteracting approaches. The final stage—transform—is when you review the effect of the counteracting approaches and make any adjustments.

Using BBM on an on-going basis, along with the more in-depth 'diagnostic' EAST process, gives you mastery over all barriers and the gift of forward focus...

A happy life
consists not in the absence
but in the mastery
of hardships

HELEN KELLER

10 Forward Focus
The Only Way To Go

Barrier Breakers: Be Yourself Brilliantly! has shown you how to live with the balance of forward focus, so your life journey will be as relaxed, successful and enjoyable as possible.

Anyone can achieve forward focus.

Forward focus is not about...

- being perfect
- having all the answers
- being 'sorted'
- achieving an end result.

Forward focus doesn't guarantee that your journey will be free from delays and diversions, that you'll never meet dangerous drivers nor have to navigate treacherous terrain. It doesn't promise that you'll never have a breakdown or breakup, never meet with accidents and disappointments, that you'll never get lost, or hit bad weather...

> There's no such thing as bad weather,
> only the wrong clothes
>
> BILLY CONNOLLY

Forward focus gives you 'the right clothes' and promises that...

- You enjoy the journey of your life.

- You move ahead while being fully in the moment.

- You recognise barriers and know how to deal with them.

- You're relaxed and ready for any challenge.

- You draw on your own potential.

- You find all the skills you need inside yourself.

- You make the most of yourself, and you help others to do the same.

- You're armed with the most practical tools, as well as the most magical...a wand of imagination to turn mundane into miraculous, a lightsaber of intuition to pierce clarity through the shadow...and more.

With forward focus you're prepared for all the thrills your journey will bring.

Enjoy it!

Be a Barrier Breaker!

And be yourself...brilliantly!

Go confidently
in the direction of your dreams.
It is time to start living the life
you've imagined

HENRY DAVID THOREAU

ABOUT THE AUTHOR

Penelope Tobin founded Barrier Breakers in 2000, a research and education charity dedicated to "inspiring human development creating positive change", and has been its creative director since that time. An expert in soft skills development and evaluation, she is creator of Barrier Breakers Methodology (BBM), which was originally presented in an RSA report (2002). Since then BBM has been applied widely throughout the UK third sector, and was recognised by the 2007 Performance Hub prize for innovative work supporting individual and organisational development. BBM has now been made available to organisations in the public and private sectors, as well as to individuals; everyone can access training and accreditation programmes through the Barrier Breakers website.

Originally an arts practitioner, Penelope Tobin started her musical career aged 18, and subsequently toured and recorded with numerous groups as a keyboard player, composed music for commercials, and led jazz ensembles–ranging from a sextet in London to a 17-piece jazz orchestra in New York. As well as being a pianist, composer, and vocalist, she is also a dedicated educator who runs workshops and coaches individuals. Her experience as an artist–educator directed the research from which BBM evolved, including an investigation into overcoming barriers to creativity, and an exploration of the relationship between the artist's way of working and twenty-first century skills needs.

She has devised and delivered numerous change programmes, advises at board level, is sought after as a speaker and facilitator of soft skills, and writes widely on the subject.

Penelope Tobin has a BA (Hons) in Performing Arts from Middlesex University, and an MA in Leading and Managing Organisational Change from City University, London. She is a Fellow of the Royal Society of Arts.

To contact the author, get additional resources, and find out about BBM training and accreditation, go to www.barrierbreakers.co.uk

Lightning Source UK Ltd.
Milton Keynes UK
UKHW022226251122
412825UK00011B/510